MEXICO

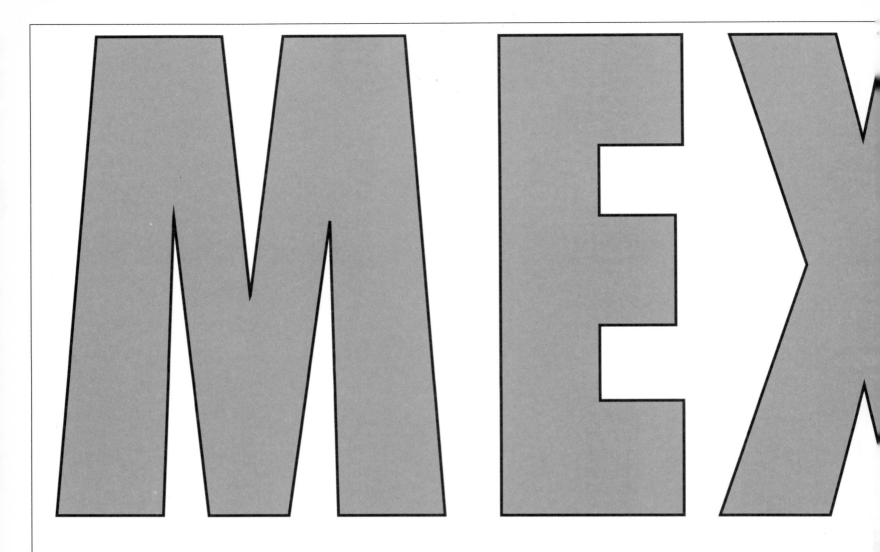

Originated and developed by

BATO TOMASEVIC

Text by

KENNETH McKENNEY

Design by

GANE ALEKSIC

A Motovun Group Book
© Flint River Press Ltd. 1992

First published in the U.K. in 1992 by
FLINT RIVER PRESS Ltd.
26 Litchfield Street, London WC2H 9NJ

ISBN: 1 871489 11 3

Distributed in Mexico by
LIBRERÍA BRITÁNICA L.A.
Serapio Rendon 125
Col. San Rafael
06470 Mexico, D.F.

Editor

Madge Phillips

Picture editor

Dieter Josef

Photographs by

Ferdinand Anders, nos. 76, 222, 239, 280–283; Ursula Bernath, nos. 17, 23, 58, 59, 61, 63, 66, 124, 127, 137, 141, 142, 169, 209–211, 215, 251, 269; Hellfied Böhm, nos. 1, 5, 27, 29, 32, 35, 41–43, 49, 56, 60, 62, 64, 75, 82, 84, 97, 98, 101–104, 106, 110, 111, 116, 122, 123, 125, 128, 130, 146, 158, 161, 167, 170, 176, 182, 196, 200, 205, 207, 221, 233, 234, 238, 241, 246, 249, 252, 254, 257–267, 271, 272, 276; Raul Dominquez, nos. 34, 191; Wolfgang Dorn, nos. 81, 139, 163, 171; Franz Ellmaier, nos. 50, 65, 67, 114; John Frost, no. 235; Maria Gornikiewicz, no. 96; Hasso Hohmann, nos. 48, 131, 157, 159, 213, 214, 224, 242, 243, 247, 248, 250, 274; Dieter Josef, nos. 3, 4, 36, 45–47, 52, 53, 72, 80, 100, 112, 115, 134, 135, 138, 148–152, 160, 195, 197, 202, 206, 212, 220, 226, 227, 235, 237, 268, 277–279; Roberto Kolb, no. 162; Ruth Letchinga-Deutsch, nos. 11–16, 18, 20, 21, 24, 28, 71, 87, 90, 91, 121; Nadine Markova, nos. 7–9, 33, 37–40, 44, 51, 70, 79, 126, 129, 132, 133, 136, 155, 165, 166, 168, 175, 177–179, 189, 198, 201, 203, 204, 208, 216, 218, 229, 231, 245; Tomas Martinez, no. 57; Rudolf Ortner, no. 275; Theo Riedl, nos. 2, 6, 10, 25, 68, 69, 83, 99, 106, 113, 117, 119, 140, 144, 181, 183, 188, 192, 230; Scala Communications Inc., nos. 89, 92–95, 217, 219, 223, 228, 240; Cristina Sequeira-Raich, no. 26; Pedro Valtierra & Co., nos. 54, 55, 73, 77, 109, 143, 145, 147, 154, 172–174, 180, 184–186, 190, 225, 232; Robert Van Der Hilst, nos. 19, 22, 30, 31, 74, 78, 85, 86, 88, 105, 118, 156, 164, 187, 193, 194, 199, 236, 244, 270, 273

The Publishers wish to express their thanks to Professor Ferdinand Anders of Vienna for his scholarly assistance, and to Dr Hellfried Böhm of the Mexican Office of the Austrian Department of Foreign Trade for his invaluable help with the pictures and for his own photographic contributions.

Type setting by Avalon

Colour separation, printing and binding
by DELO - Tiskarna, Ljubljana, Slovenia

CONTENTS

8

THE LAND AND ITS PEOPLE

Trumpet in the Sea. South of the Border. In the Curve of the Gulf. A Slice of
Pacific Coast. Playgrounds of the Rich. The Heartland.

54

EARLY CIVILIZATIONS

Tepexpan, the Elephant Man. The Miller's Tale. The Dancers of Tlatilco. The
Missionaries. Olmecs, the Big Heads. Teotihuacán, City of Ghosts.

92

ANCIENT EMPIRES

The Aztecs, the Sun Warriors. The Lake City of Tenochtitlan. The Maya,
Lords of Darkness and Light. The Conquest: Arrival of the Horse–Gods.

133

NEW SPAIN

The Cleaning of the Slate. The Years of Plunder.
The Break with Spain.

157

INDEPENDENCE

The New Republic. The French Connection. War with the United States.
Juárez and Maximilian.

198

REVOLUTION

The Turn of Porfirio Díaz. A Decade of Bloodshed.
Obregón, the Practical President.

207

VISIONS AND REALITY

The Revolution's Legacy. Trouble with the Neighbours.
Bearing the Cross.

246

THE MEXICAN WAY

The Showmen. The Fixers, Sacred and Profane.
A Moveable Feast.

286
CHRONOLOGY

288
INDEX

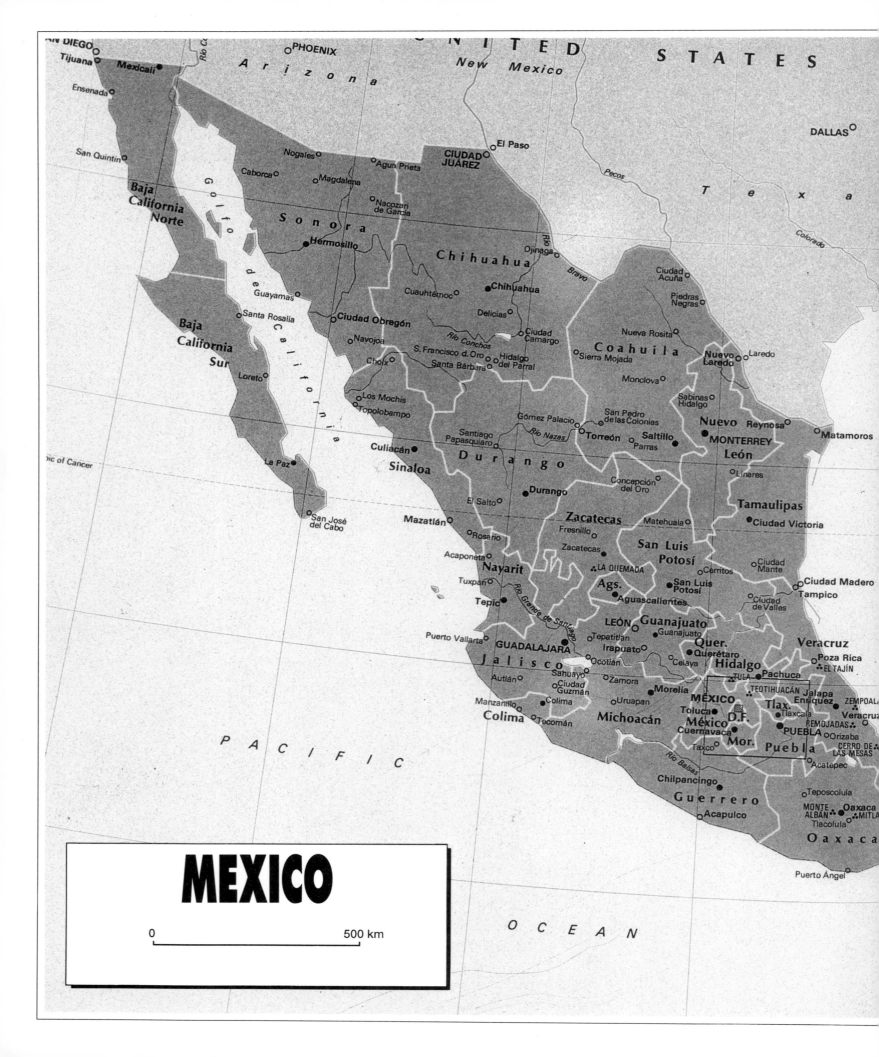

MEXICO

0   500 km

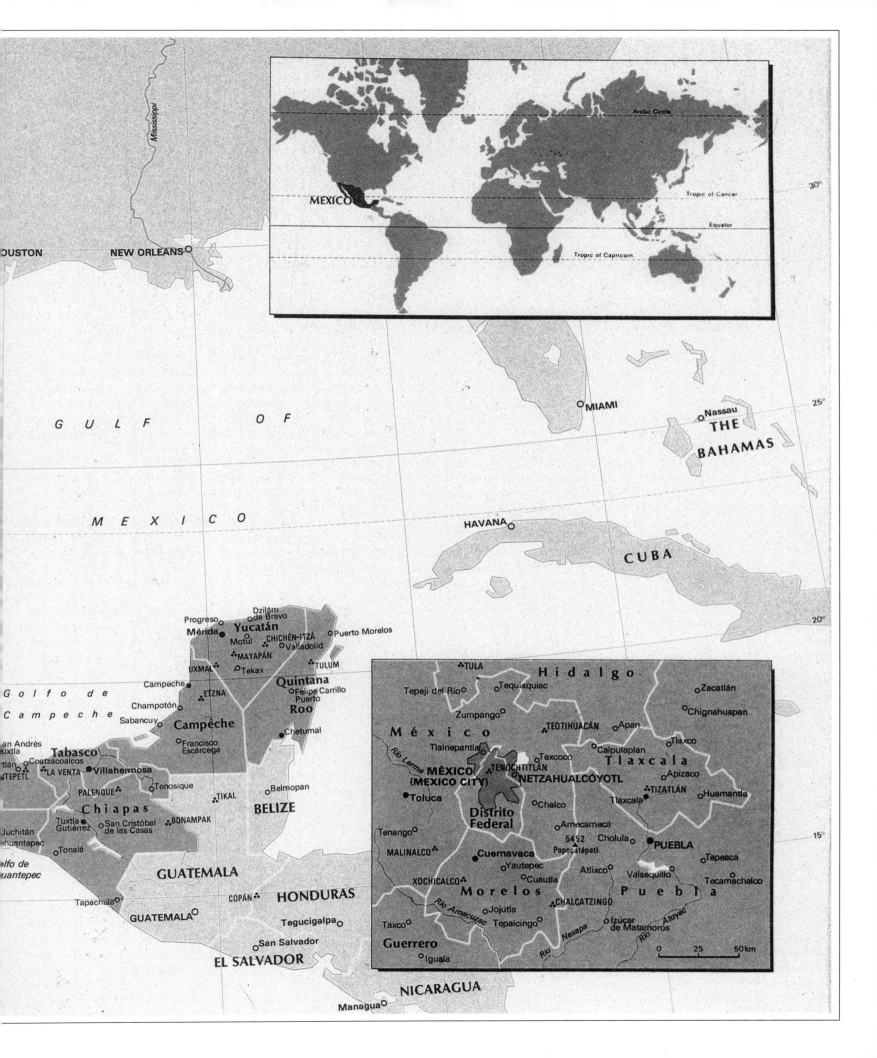

HOUSTON

NEW ORLEANS○

Mississippi

MEXICO

Arctic Circle

Tropic of Cancer

Equator

Tropic of Capricorn

30°

G U L F   *O F*

○ MIAMI

Nassau○

THE

BAHAMAS

25°

M E X I C O

HAVANA○

CUBA

20°

Progreso○   Dzilám
de Bravo○

Mérida○   **Yucatán**○   ○Puerto Morelos
            Motul○   **CHICHÉN-ITZÁ**
                        Valladolid○
              ◆**MAYAPÁN**
Golfo d e   **UXMAL**○   ○Tekax
              Quintana
C a m p e c h e   Campeche●   ○Felipe Carrillo
                                  Puerto
   Champotón○   ◆ETZNA   **Roo**
   Sabancuy○   **Campéche**   **TULUM**
an Andrés
uxtla○   ○Francisco   Chetumal●
tlán○   Escárcega
NTEPETL○ **Tabasco**
  Coatzacoalcos○
  ○**LA VENTA** ○Villahermosa
                              ○Belmopan
PALENQUE♣   ○Tenosique
           Chiapas   ◆**TIKAL**
Juchitán○   **BELIZE**
huantepec Tuxtla○ ○San Cristóbal
          Gutiérrez de las Casas ◆**BONAMPAK**
lfo de
uantepec ○Tonalá
              GUATEMALA
                         COPÁN♣ **HONDURAS**
 Tapachula○
  GUATEMALA○   Tegucigalpa○

San Salvador○

EL SALVADOR

15°

NICARAGUA

Managua○

(inset map, lower right)

♣**TULA**   **H i d a l g o**
Tepeji del Río○   ○Tequixquiac   ○Zacatlán

M é x i c o   ♣**TEOTIHUACÁN** ○Apan   ○Chignahuapan
 Zumpango○   ○Tlaxco
        Tlalnepantla○   ○Texcoco   **T l a x c a l a**
Río Lerma **MÉXICO** ◆**TENOCHTITLÁN** ○Calpulalpan ○Apizaco
          (MEXICO CITY) **NETZAHUALCÓYOTL** ♣**TIZATLÁN**
                                        Tlaxcala○   ○Huamantla
        ●Toluca   ○Chalco
   Tenango○   **Distrito**
                  Federal   ○Amecameca
MALINALCO♣   5452 Cholula○
                        Popocatépetl ●**PUEBLA**
                  ●Cuernavaca   ○Tepeaca
   XOCHICALCO♣ ○Yautepec   Atlixco○ Valsequillo○ Tecamachalco○
                  ○Cuautla
              M o r e l o s   ♣**CHALCATZINGO**   **P u e b l a**
        Taxco○   *Río Amacuzac* ○Jojutla ○Izúcar
                        Tepalcingo○ de Matamoros *Atoyac*
 Guerrero   *Nexapa* *Río*
        ○Iguala

0   25   50km

The Land and its People

Trumpet in the Sea

Mexico lies like a huge trumpet between the Pacific Ocean and the Gulf of Mexico – its mouthpiece washed by the Carribean. It is a trumpet not unlike those used by the Aztecs or the Maya at times of war or celebration. It is a trumpet that blows north, toward America, toward Europe. And that is where new settlers have always come from, those who responded to its call, to change the land and its civilizations for ever.

The mouthpiece is the east coast of the Yucatán Peninsula, running from Cabo Catoche to the border of Belize; from open limestone country, the home of cactus and succulants, to steaming green jungle that covers the earth like a blanket. If you take a mask and snorkle into the clear crystalline waters near Isla Mujeres, an island just to the north of Yucatán, in the early dawn and sink into the warm, glass-like shallows, you may see parrot fish the size of turtles gnawing the raw coral. Turtles swim there too, as do rays flying bat-like across the sandy sea-bed. With their myriad fish and coral reefs, these translucent waters, an amazing turquoise hue, are a paradise for snorkeling and scuba diving.

The seas off Mexico teem with fish of all shapes and sizes, with life, with activity. As does Mexico itself. It is a land of colour and movement, a land of images, some of which never leave the mind. And, always, history surrounds you. In every tile or brick, shard of pottery, splash of paint, there is a message from the past: part Indian, part Spanish, mainly a mixture of both.

As the body of Mexico's trumpet curls up, widens, to the north, it is shaped by two great mountain chains, the Sierra Madre Oriental and the Sierra Madre Occidental, massive barriers rising from six to twelve thousand feet in a series of peaks. In the centre, between the chains, is high, irregular tableland. Flying over its browns and reds and dusty yellows, one gets the impression of a landscape moulded by the elements. Wind, rain and searing heat have skinned the earth, leaving bone and muscle exposed, yet it remains a living entity. As one drives through it, the patch of dust ahead turns into a leathery farmer following his wooden plough drawn by a mule.

The heart of Mexico is the capital, the most densely populated metropolis on this planet. The latest estimate gives the population as twenty million. If the birthrate remains unchanged, it is calculated that by the end of this century Mexico City will have thirty million inhabitants. There are plans to correct this congestion, the pollution, and the concentration of industry that plague the city today. Perhaps some of them will be successfully implemented. The current President has radical plans for the future: the old peasant landholding system is being broken down, foreign investment is being encouraged, the State is coming to terms with the Church.

The trumpet bell of Mexico faces the U.S.A. and the two thousand or so miles of border separating one country from the other. Following the line of rivers and cutting across deserts, it runs from San Diego on the west coast to Matamoros on the east. Each major junction along the border has two names, one Mexican, the other used by the Americans. On the northern side Matamoros becomes Brownsville; Nuevo Laredo, Laredo; Ciudad Juárez, El Paso; and Tijuana and San Diego run together. The Mexicans call the great river flowing east to the Gulf of Mexico the Bravo del Norte; to the Americans it is the Rio Grande.

The Mexicans and the Americans often have different ways of expressing, naming, calling attention to what is often essentially the same event. Take, for example, one of the items that daily crops up at the border: the countless numbers of undocumented workers seeking hope in the U.S.A., Mexicans willing to work for a basic minimum of about three to four dollars an hour, the equivalent of what they would earn per day at

1. Acapulco divers swoop like swallows from the cliffs into a narrow cove where the rocks are knife-edged. Watched by tourists from all over the world, they carry their lives in their outspread arms as they plunge into the Pacific waves.

2. The volcano Paracutín came up in a farmer's field in the state of Michoacán in 1943. The farmer is said to have kicked the blaze in an attempt to put it out. He failed. The cone rose to some 1200 feet and smoulders still. (pp. 10-11)

3. Popocatépetl, the Sentinel, and his companion volcano, Ixtacíhuatl, the Sleeping Lady, are said to have been fleeing lovers. According to legend, while resting for the night they became frozen and have remained there ever since, but one day Popocatépetl will rise, wake his companion, and lead her to their paradise. (pp. 12-13)

4. *Giant cactus in Sonoran light. Sonora produces most of Mexico's wheat, much of its fruit and a lot of copper. Yet it is bare of people. The three Californian Gulf states, Nayarit, Sinaloa and Sonora, make up over 20 per cent of the landmass, but have only six per cent of the population.*

5. *A village tucked away among the folded hills in Chacaltzingo, state of Morelos. Wall carvings discovered here were probably the work of the Olmecs, who spread their culture throughout the land before the Spaniards came.* (*pp. 16-17*)

6. *Barranca de Cobre, Copper Canyon, the hard, dry, weather-beaten country of the north-west. With its dust, its cover, its labyrinth of gulches, it is the sort of place where Pancho Villa rode at the height of his fame. (pp. 18-19)*

7 . *Mexico's Pacific Coast, where stalky coconut palms frame the sky, is justly renowned for its tourist resorts: Acapulco, Ixtapa, Puerto Villarta... The latest to join them is Huatulco, due for completion in 2020. (pp. 20-21)*

8. *Cabo San Luca, at the end of Baja California, once a shelter for pirates, is now a busy international resort. Life here has changed dramatically, but not these majestic cliffs rising from the waves. (pp. 22-23)*

home. To the Americans they are wetbacks, because some of them cross the Rio Grande to arrive sodden on the other side. To the Mexicans they are *pollos*, chickens, often herded, cooped and parcelled across the frontier by men who earn their living that way. Such men are called coyotes on both sides of the border.

Also passing between these two countries, the United States of America and the United States of Mexico, are millions of gallons of oil each year – there have been times when Mexico topped the list of American suppliers. Thousands of tons of crops and merchandise are likewise sent north, the latter ranging from shoes to auto parts. The crops are not those one might expect – the corn and beans for which Mexico is famous – but more luxurious fare that the Americans can afford, like strawberries, asparagus and broccoli, and also colourful gladioli. Mexico, in turn, imports much of its basic foods, like corn and beans: many of the tortillas in Mexico City are made with imported corn. This is just one of the countless surprises and paradoxes that this land of contrasts holds in store.

Mexico as a country has an area of some eight hundred thousand square miles. It is vast, varied, magical, mystical, and yet earthy and alive. It is made up of a Federal District, in which Mexico City lies, twenty-nine states and two territories, each different, distinct and in its own way remarkable. Each state has its own governor and legislature, but in all but one case, the governor belongs to the ruling party, the PRI. It is a country that is politically tightly-bound.

South of the Border

Baja California, split administratively into two states, Norte and Sur, is a long arm of land stretching down into the Pacific, with some sixty thousand square miles of what is mostly mountain chain, impressive deserts and endless coastline.

In the north of Baja (Lower) California are the steamy frontier towns of Tijuana and Mexicali, melting pots on the edges of divergent cultures, with all the mixture that such proximity to the U.S. implies.

Tijuana, which grew up around a ranch called Tia Juana in the 1840s, became famous mainly thanks to Herb Alpert and his Tijuana Brass, whose records of mock-Mexican music were world-wide best-sellers in the 1960s. The town became popular with Americans in the Prohibition era, for obvious reasons. Mexicans have never banned, nor seen the need to ban, alcohol. The tradition of easy-come, easy-go, has persisted. There is a fine horse racing track in Tijuana; Jai Alai contests and bullfights are held. It has an open border zone, extending south for some fifteen miles, where tourists come and go without the need for visas or any other documents.

Mexicali, the capital of Baja California Norte, is a hot, dense, industrial town whose principal business is taking care of tourists. It is said to have the highest standard of living, as a city, in the whole of Mexico. Much of its wealth comes from the handling of cotton, grown in the flatlands on either side of the Sierra de Juárez mountains. Much of it comes also from the 'In-Bond' agreement between the United States and Mexico, a convenient arrangement by which materials are brought south by Americans to be assembled by Mexican hands, a tax-exempt deal without border duties, customs fees or other demands. This means that many Mexicans receive wages they might not otherwise come by, and American manufacturers have a constant source of cheap labour. The finished goods are then returned for sale in the U.S.A.

9. A tumbling waterfall in the high country above the slopes of Veracruz. Mexico offers astonishing scenic diversity, from the hard, dry north, through the snow-covered peaks above Mexico City, to the mist-enshrouded jungles of Chiapas.

Teotihuacán: High priest of Tláloc,
god of water.

Vegetation and wildlife in Baja California are, as might be expected, somewhat limited by the configuration of the land and the climate. The mountains carry forests, mainly of pine. Below these is scrubland, descending to the coast, to the warm, soft water. Animal life is sparse, consisting mainly of various species of rats – long-eared, desert and others, reptiles, and the famous coyotes. In contrast, the birdlife of Baja California is prolific, thanks to the miles of coastline, the swamps and miasmas, and attracts many hunters. In high country, hawks and eagles may be seen, although in decreasing numbers. At lower altitudes there are partridge, duck and other waterfowl; swallows and martins flicker in the sun.

And there is a lot of sun in Baja California. Most of the jagged peninsula is hot, parched desert with cactus, stretches of rock and sand.

In the south, near the tip of the peninsula, stands the state capital, La Paz, a tourist resort on a lagoon. The area offers vast expanses of dazzling white sand, wonderful fishing, and a sense of isolation from the rest of the country, lying as it does at the end of this six-hundred-mile-long peninsula and across the Sea of Cortés from the mainland.

Chihuahua, the state, is nearly one hundred thousand square miles of what is mainly desert, cactus land, patches of mezquite, apart from bare, outcropping rock. You could put England into Chihuahua twice and there would still be a little left over.

In ancient times, that is to say, before the Spaniards came, Chihuahua was occupied by nomadic bands of hunters living off small game such as kangaroo rats and hare, scratching some sustenance from wild plants and roots that grew in the more humid valleys. Such people were called Chichimec, Sons of Dogs. Canine associations with this region would appear to go a long way back.

Today, the city of Chihuahua, the state capital, is a mining centre: zinc, lead, copper and gold are all extracted in the area. It is also a focal point for cattle dealing. Livestock is raised in valley-ranches, on cooler mountain slopes where there is enough grazing and water to sustain them.

It was in Chihuahua that Pancho Villa, one of the leaders of Mexico's revolution, joined the forces that took him to war. Born in the neighbouring state of Durango in 1877, Villa became an outlaw at the age of sixteen, after killing a landowner's son who had raped his sister. He changed his name (from Doroteo Arango), joined a mountain outlaw band, and in 1909 was recruited to the revolutionary forces by Abraham Gonzalez in the city of Chihuahua.

Somewhat incongruously, the name of the city and state is best known abroad because of a toy dog. The tiny terrier-like Chihuahua – average shoulder height five inches – is descended from the ninth-century Techichi, a dog of the Central American Indian group, the Toltecs. It is known that another Indian culture, the Maya, ate dogs, considering them a delicacy, so the Toltecs may have done the same. Perhaps it was the little ones that escaped attention and went on to become the pets they are today. Perhaps it is the climate, but a Chihuahua has a body temperature of 104 degrees Fahrenheit – a genuinely hot dog.

'Chihuahua!' has become a Mexican expletive, a harmless oath, taking the place of a stronger curse, used when something irritates or to express mild wonder. For a more vexing or acrimonious situation, Mexicans have a vivid and imaginative range of curses, of which the most common and effective is *pendejo* (a pubic hair). In a country where a macho image is widely cultivated, to be called a *pendejo* is an insult indeed.

Tamaulipas, the only one of the Gulf-coast states bordering on the U.S.A., is large, mountainous to the west, and arid. Cactus blooms, in higher country pines grow, and down along the coast are swamplands, lagoons and harsh grasses. Here begins the great sweep of shoreline that runs all the way to the Yucatán Peninsula, the sickle-shape of mangroves, palms and spiny bushes, backed by rich orchards of citrus fruits, sugar-cane plantations and cornfields. Off shore, the rich fishing grounds of the Gulf of Mexico with their shoals of mackerel and banks of shrimp now sprout oil rigs that deliver far greater wealth.

Ciudad Victoria, an inland city and centre of trade, agriculture and the mining industries, is the capital of Tamaulipas. Better known abroad is the main port, Tampico, halfway down the Gulf coast, at the mouth of the Pánuco River. Its harbour is busy with ships that range from oil tankers to small fishing boats, from natural gas containers to trawlers that go out with net or long line. Oil was first discovered in the area in 1910. The Spanish settled here in 1522, when Cortés founded a town, Pánuco, on the river. And way back in time, over a thousand years ago, the Huastecs, fathers of the Aztec Empire, had their kingdom in this region.

Matamoros, close to the eastern end of the Mexican-U.S. border, is part of the same urban mix as Brownsville on the American side. To cross from one to the other is easy – a taxi ride without a glance from customs officials if you stay within the free border area.

In the Curve of the Gulf

Veracruz, Tabasco and Campeche are the three states that complete the huge sickle-side of Mexico that curves south and then north around the Gulf of Mexico. They are, in the main, narrow states lying between the mountains and the sea. The further south you go, the softer the air becomes; the further south you go, the more distant becomes the grasping heat of Tamaulipas. That is until you reach the great flat limestone tablelands of Campeche. They will lead you to Yucatán, where warm winds blow once more, where the cactus begins again.

Veracruz, one of the chief fruit-growing states of Mexico, is an area steeped in history. It was on this stretch of Gulf coastline that Cortés landed with his fleet in 1519 and soon after founded a city, named Veracruz (True Cross), since Good Friday had been chosen as the official foundation day. This city is now Mexico's biggest port.

Its shores have heard the swish of paddles of Indian canoes, the creak of rigging of Spanish galleons, the rattle of gunboats when United States forces captured the port in 1847, during the war between the U.S.A. and Mexico, and again in 1914, when Veracruz was once more occupied by the Americans.

The jungles of Veracruz, once plagued by yellow fever, have seen the passing of many feet. Cortés came this way with his company of conquistadores when he set off toward Montezuma and Tenochtitlán, the city that was to become México. Other Spaniards followed. Merchants developed roads and carriageways. Veracruz connected Mexico with Spain. From the Gulf of Mexico out into the Atlantic, galleons carried all they could from the new country to the old. Spain became so dependent on gold and other riches from the new American territories that when the sources began to dry so, in many ways, did Spain itself.

In the nineteenth century railroad engineers carved their tracks through the steaming jungles. The first contract for a rail line was granted in 1837 – to link Veracruz with Mexico City.

Today the railroad runs, cars fill the roads, the feet of tourists tramp stretches that were once the province of jaguars. The jaguars have almost gone, but remains of them can be seen in museums – the splendid cloaks once worn by Maya lords who also passed this way.

Tabasco, whence the chili-sauce got its name, extends the littoral curve below the Gulf of Mexico. As the land stretches to the east the jungles thin, mahogany and cedar give way to less noble woods. The earth is wetter. Swamps, lagoons and broad river-mouths spread over the coastal plains.

Rubber is tapped there, bananas grow, as do pineapples, and chickle – the goo that used to form the basis for chewing-gum. Nowadays chickle has been replaced by polyvinyl acetate, a synthetic polymer, which somehow seems to lack the magic of the gum from the giant sapodilla tree, whose leaves were once used by pirates as playing cards – dried and marked with symbols.

Chewing-gum, in the form of chickle, was introduced to us by the Mexican general, Antonio López de Santa Anna, before he attacked the Alamo in Texas, where Davy Crockett and Jim Bowie died. General Santa Anna, a chickle-chewer, gave a sample of his favourite chew to Thomas Adams, American photographer and inventor. The rest, as they say, is history.

Tabasco sauce, on the other hand, has little to do with Mexico. It was invented by another American, Edmund McIlhenny, who called it Tabasco because he liked the sound of the name.

Long before Tabasco sauce was ever thought of, an early group of Mexican Indians, the Olmecs, constructed their greatest ceremonial site on an island in the centre of a mangrove swamp in the northern part of Tabasco. Here, somewhere about 1000 BC, they prayed to their particular gods and left for us to discover, at La Venta, some of the finest jade carvings ever found in Mexico. And some of the biggest carved heads in the world, which once stared out over the shallow Campeche waters.

Campeche is close to my heart.

Driving into Campeche one evening, through quite typical pouring rain, my eye was taken by the massive fortifications along the waterfront of the town. Massive stone walls, like those of a medieval fortress, protected the heart of the old city, their flat, difficult-to-scale faces turned to the sea.

It was my first visit to Campeche and nobody had warned me what to expect. In many ways this was fortunate. I felt as if I had discovered something on my own, and this fascination with the presence of an unexpected link with the past led to my second novel about Mexico, *These Kingdoms*, published in 1987.

The battlements of Campeche were built, mainly in the seventeenth

Teotihuacán: Procession of coyotes and jaguars, mural.

28

century, to discourage pirate assaults. From its earliest days the port of Campeche had been open to attack; any pirate worth his salt had sailed in through the shallow seas, sacked the town, taken what he could from it, often burning what was left.

Henry Morgan left his mark on Campeche, so did Bartholomew the Portuguese. Francis Drake seized vessels outward bound from Campeche, as did Rock Brasiliano and Robert Chevalier, the Frenchman. They came from every country that could put a ship to sea. They took the gold and silver, itself taken from the Indians, and claimed it as their own. They have gone. Their monument, the fortress-face of Campeche, remains solid to this day.

And something else. As the Spanish authorities in Campeche became more desperate in their efforts to protect their town – before the battlements were complete – they learned how to deal with the pirates, the plunderers, the burners, the hostage-takers. They learned to trade. So much gold or silver meant that nothing burned; so much oil, salt-beef or pork meant that fewer women were abducted – or that those who were came from a less important sector of town, a mulatto, perhaps, a mestiza without a protector.

There is little romance in piracy, banditry, and the like. In order to endure, from time to time all that remains is to make a deal – however distasteful it might seem. Mexico has survived with this reality.

Fortifications in Campeche were not restricted to the town: the earliest battlements in the whole of Mexico were discovered in Becán, a site near the Guatemala border. These ruins, surrounded by a moat, date from about 500 BC. (Defence, in Campeche, goes back a long way.) It is one of the sites of the many castles people built in order to survive in the violent past.

Today, the wildlife and vegetation in Veracruz, Tabasco and Campeche remain a mixture of what the Indians knew and that grafted on by others. The splendid hardwood trees are now much depleted. As you go further east, up onto the flat-capped limestone of Yucatán, the cactus and the grasslands have scarcely changed. The jaguar has almost vanished, but badgers can be found in the dark woodlands, burrowed deep beneath the protecting earth, a defence that has secured their survival.

If we turn west from Campeche, leaving behind the waters of the Gulf, we traverse the trumpet-neck of Mexico, crossing the highland state of *Chiapas*. Flying over its black and brilliant green, its defying camouflage, the airborne traveller is unaware that beneath its cover are Indian tribes that have hardly changed their ways. Like the badger they have burrowed.

Chiapas is large – some thirty thousand square miles – and mainly mountainous. It shares a border with Guatemala and for many years was part of that country. In the early nineteenth century, when Mexico gained its independence from Spain, Chiapas belonged to Guatemala. Later it decided to become part of the United States of Mexico, and this change of loyalty has lent a sense of isolation to this lush state that has never been quite resolved. Many Guatemalans still think of Chiapas as their own.

Deep in the jungle, hidden behind walls of vine and creeper, there are villages that belong to another age. The inhabitants of these villages are Indians. In their dirt-floor huts, which have neither electricity nor plumbing, not a word of Spanish is heard. Their language is a version of that spoken by the ancient Zapotecs, by all accounts a fairly peaceful tribe living in the broad fertile valley of Oaxaca, a state that borders on Chiapas on the west. They also inhabited the mountains of Chiapas, the lower leg of the Sierra Madre, where their descendants can be found today, behind their jungle curtain.

The Zapotecs built the majestic temple complex at Monte Albán in neighbouring Oaxaca, where what they had established was later added to by others. These were not the only ambitious builders in this part of Mexico. The Maya, with their highly developed society of lords and priests and warriors, with their sense of time and destiny, built in the jungles of Chiapas their magnificent city of Palenque, a temple centre more than a dwelling place, a site of bloody rites. Palenque, set in the green-clad northern lowlands of the state, has been described as a city that shines with a splendour few others can match. Discovered in the eighteeenth century, it has been partially restored, and today, walking through the ruins, you can turn a corner and almost see the form of a splendid Maya warrior striding across a flagstone courtyard. What your eye has caught is one of the many bas-relief figures carved in stone.

The city of Palenque once covered an area of some thirty acres. The temples, dwelling houses, and layered walkways were built on high pyramidal settings in a jungle so thick it seems to be impenetrable. It is calculated that the best work in Palenque was done in the last half of the seventh century and the early years of the eighth.

John Lloyd Stephens, the American archaeologist who examined and worked on more Maya sites than any other explorer in his field, tried to buy Palenque in the 1840s for fifteen hundred US dollars but, because he was a foreigner not married to a Mexican, he was unable to complete the deal. It is not recorded if he contemplated taking a Mexican wife with Palenque as her dowry.

No one knows why the Maya left Palenque. In fact no one is sure why the great and powerful Maya race, with all their skills and talents and knowledge, passed from their seats of power.

We will look at this and the other important Mexican archaeological sites in a later section. To keep Palenque in mind until then, we might recall the line by Percy Bysshe Shelley in *Ozymandias of Egypt*, referring to glorious ruin: 'Look on my works, ye Mighty, and despair!'

A Slice of Pacific Coast

In the state of *Oaxaca*, pronounced Wa-ha-ka, the ancient Zapotecs carved their mountains, the greatest of which is Monte Albán. Here, in the soft, warm climate, they crafted hilltops as shrines to their gods. Here, thousands of Indian hands turned the landscape into the shape of their belief.

If you fly from Mexico City to Oaxaca, the flight path crosses the mountain top. On a clear day you can see the grandest ceremonial layout in all Mexico. Below, lies a huge stretch of land flattened by Zapotecan labour. From it rise the stepped pyramids of the holy shrines with their broad stairways and their clear sharp lines. Just for a moment or two you might imagine the turning back of time – those ant-like figures walking the ruins could be Zapotecs, going about their business before the birth of Christ. Then the magic ceases, reality returns, the figures are tourists, their heads turned up in wonder.

Not everything in Oaxaca is built on so grand a scale. In the city of Oaxaca, seated beneath the awning of a sidewalk café with a glass of excellent Mexican beer, you are quite likely to see Indian women pass – so small they do not quite reach the height of the parking metres they negotiate on their way to a central square where they weave their brilliant fabrics.

Black and red are the principal colours of the cloth they produce, the methods the same as those of their ancestors who walked the pathways of Monte Albán. The women sit holding part of the cloth they have woven with their feet. The shafts and shuttles they use are primitive – and they have vast numbers of them. They will sell half-finished wall hangings, loom and all, so that you can buy not only the art itself but the means of production.

The work they produce is beautiful. As they create they talk, weaving a fabric of their sound, a chattering of a native tongue. It seems the only words of Spanish they have are those needed to clinch a bargain.

Oaxaca, however, has produced more than splendid ruins and close-woven, brightly-coloured cloth. Two of Mexico's best known presidents – one loved, one hated – were born in the state. Both left their indelible stamp on Mexico. One was a democrat, severe but attempting to be fair, the other a more genial dictator who sold Mexico to foreign investors and had the world blow up in his face.

Benito Juárez, president from 1858 to 1872, was a Zapotec Indian with no trace of European blood. Porfirio Díaz, president from 1876 to 1880, and again from 1884 to 1911, was lighter-skinned, although he had, in part, Mixtec Indian ancestry. Juárez was loved, idolized almost, because he was from the people and for the people. Díaz, when he gained power, abandoned Juárez's democratic policy in favour of economic development, giving power and wealth to those who served him. Congress was appointed from his friends. Díaz became a feared and detested man. His policies led to the Mexican Revolution of 1910, the revolution that gave shape to the Mexico we know today. We will meet both these men again when we look at Mexican history in greater detail.

Wildlife and vegetation in Oaxaca and neighbouring Chiapas, especially in the higher, forest-clad outbacks, are rich and varied. In the valleys acacias and cypress grow alongside the tall, spike-leaved yuccas and other cacti. Here, rabbits, squirrels and shrews abound. These are peaceful valleys that could easily belong to some European landscape.

Nuño de Guzmán, governor of Pánuco, conquered New Galicia (northwestern Mexico).

31

Higher, in the pine and conifer forests, the wildlife is less visible, although the occasional white-tailed deer may be seen disappearing into a shadier darkness. And in the evenings, especially in Chiapas, toward the Guatemala border, spider monkeys are heard as they rustle through tree tops, and are sometimes seen hanging in the twilight. Then, in a moment, they turn and swing away.

And you have the time, before craning to catch sight of another, to scratch at your mosquito bites and slap on more insect-repellent. There is every sort of insect life. During the day, when a beautiful butterfly settles on a flower, or a dragonfly, bronze and green and golden, hangs shimmering over water, it is to be wondered at. At night, as a mosquito hums whiningly into your ear as you try to sleep, you wonder where it fits into the scheme of things at all.

Birdlife is plentiful. At times the air seems full of small feathered creatures, nuthatches, tits of all shapes and sizes, bluebirds, flycatchers, doves and pigeons.

And now and then, deep in the forests, you may catch a glimpse of the most spectacular bird in Mexico, in the whole of the New World. It is the trogon, the resplendent quetzal, whose long emerald-green tail feathers were so treasured by the ancient Maya. The Maya trapped these splendid creatures by the thousand, and plucked out their tail feathers to present to their lords. In fact, the bird's tail is white; what was sought after were the two-foot-long uppertail coverts. Great cloaks were made of these trophies; the lords wore them, died in them, were often wrapped in them as they were laid in their tombs. Some remain today, on the walls of museums.

The bird itself is now rare – rare and exotic, like much else in this part of Mexico, a section of the country that has been left behind, encapsulated in its own particular time. Like the parrots and parakeets, also seen in the tall deciduous trees of the lowland forests, Chiapas and Oaxaca are vivid, somehow timeless, patches of colour in what can often be a dry and hungry landscape.

Playgrounds of the Rich

Beach states swirl up along the coast of western Mexico, washed by the Pacific Ocean. North of them is the Golfo de California, the long, mainly shallow, waterway between the arm of Baja California and the body of Mexico.

Although in many ways they differ, all these states share similar climates, all have foothills – skirts, the Mexican text-books call them – running down from the great Sierra Madre Occidental or its footplate, the Sierra Madre del Sur, to the sea.

The climate is temperate and fairly dry. In summer it is hot, with days of endless sunshine; in winter milder, damper, but always pleasant. This is one reason why world-famous tourist resorts like Acapulco, Ixtapa and Puerto Vallarta have grown up along the coastline.

Acapulco is in the state of *Guerrero*, another large, meagrely-populated chunk of Mexico. Apart from the narrow coastal plain, it is broken, mountainous and rich in minerals such as silver, copper and zinc. Although silver has been mined in Guerrero for years, much of the rest of the mineral potential has been left untapped owing to the ruggedness of the terrain.

Acapulco, of course, has always been a goldmine. Since it was founded by the Spanish in 1550 as a Pacific port linking New Spain, as Mexico was then known, with the Philippines, a further Spanish colony,

11. Market squares, where women meet to barter, sell, select and gossip, are vital points of contact in the mingling of Mexican cultures. Ancient craft products are often sold or exchanged for plastic buckets or children's toys.

12. Gathered in a highland village, they have come to visit a curandera, the local herbal dealer, who with her leaves and potions, egg yolks and spells, often inspires more faith than any qualified medical practitioner.

13. *Bargaining, bartering, saving a peso or two, are part of the life of the marketplace. Heart-rending expressions, like this, are all part of the process. When a price is agreed for a bag, a basket, a sample of splendid embroidery, the smiles return. Simple proof that a friendly interchange has been achieved.*

14. In spite of an oil boom, millions of tourists, and satellite TV, parts of Mexico have hardly been touched by the outside world. These faces, staring out of a Chiapan scrub, belong deeply, steadily, to the past.

15. Suspended between past and present, these women from Veracruz proudly display their handwoven skirts before the invading camera as they stand beside their thatched dwelling.

16 . An Otomi woman from the
highlands in the state of Mexico weaving
in the age-old fashion. If the implements
seem crude, the results are often
amazingly rich and colourful. The
primitive shafts and shuttles used to
weave the fabric may be sold as part of
the wall-hanging.

17. Mexico has been likened to a series of villages knitted together as a nation. The variety of language, customs and handicraft forms are all quoted as evidence of this. Some villages produce basketwork, others masks or pottery. Chiconcuac, north-east of Mexico City, is noted for its needlework, sarapes and blankets. The carpets are from Temoaya in the state of Mexico.

18. Down through the centuries, Mexican women have carried their babies on their backs in rebozos – shawls that leave the hands free for toil, and can be pulled over the head to keep out rain and cold. When there is no child to be carried, the rebozo may serve as a shopping basket or as a bag for firewood.

19. Mexican children are much loved and well cared for. Even among the very poor they are often indulged. These two children, dressed in their finest huipiles, wearing their necklaces of multi-coloured beads, wait patiently for Mamá to take them out.

20, 21. *Oaxaca, the city below the mountaintop where the Zapotecs and the Mixtecs sculpted Monte Albán, is a centre of fine needlework, of delicate embroidery. The designs and dyes, like the languages spoken by the women who produce the work, go back to the times when their ancestors built their shrines and buried their dead with beautiful gifts for the after-life.*

22. *Reds, greens, yellows, black and gold are all part of the spectrum of this huipil, a shift-like garment that has been worn across a band of southern Mexico since the Indians first settled there. The colours echo the brilliant hues of the jungle parrots and the gorgeous tail-feathers of the quetzal bird, prized by the ancient Maya more than gold.*

23. *Spinning, weaving and embroidery have been finely developed Indian arts since the time of the Aztecs, Toltecs and Maya. The costume work of old has left its stamp. This woman from Zacatecas in the northern highlands, famous for its sarapes, shows how well the skills have travelled down through the ages.*

24. *Mexican handicrafts have survived all the changes, social and political, that have swept the country in the past century or two. This woman from San Andres, Jalisco, wears and displays the wool she has worked from the first spinning to the final stitch.*

25. From earliest times Mexican women have dressed colourfully, taking as their inspiration the bird life and the carpets of flowers that blossom after rain. Clay figurines depicting some of the first settlements in the Valley of Mexico show women with rouge on their cheeks and adorned with long ropes of heavy jewelry.

27. A Totonac man from Veracruz, member of another group that speaks its own language. Dressed to perform the Flight of the Eagle, he will climb the pole and, tied by his feet, spin slowly down to earth.

26. Three Tzotzil men in Chamula, Chiapas, wearing coarse woollen tunics, baggy cotton pantaloons and splendid sombreros with tassels and bindings of felt. The Tzotzils speak their own language and practise secret religious ceremonies formed around the Holy Trinity and their native beliefs that go back beyond the coming of Christianity.

Acapulco has been a valued part of Mexico. Then galleons made annual trips to and from Manilla.

In the sixteenth century Spanish galleons, sails billowing, holds often crammed with bales of silk, sailed for eight or ten or fourteen weeks from the Philippines to Acapulco. They returned in much the same amount of time, frequently carrying silver to pay for the silk. Today tourists fly, in a matter of hours, with little more than a swimsuit or a bikini, a bottle of sun-tan lotion, to spend a week or two in the sun. They return bronzed, touched by Acapulco gold, often with much to store in the holds of their memories, with much to polish in the warehouses of their dreams.

I stayed in a dream house, once, in Acapulco.

It was a multi-layered, many-roomed, elegant mansion set high on a cliff overlooking a broad sweep of the Pacific Ocean. Long white walkways, with floor tiles in reds, oranges, subtle browns, led from one section of the house to another, gracious archways opened onto dining rooms, sitting rooms, calm corners.

Servants moved quietly and were always there.

It was a house out of a movie set, and so it should have been – it was owned by a film producer in Mexico City.

Below it, after passing beneath banana palms and giant mango trees, walking down a hundred steps, you came to a natural swimming pool crafted out of the coastline. Where it joined the sea was a shark-fence to keep out intruders, whatever form they came in. The whole dwelling was walled, protected from the outside world. It was a place to visit, not to live in. It was a place to sit in briefly and quietly close the mind.

Mexico is a country of enormous contrasts, but there can be few other places where these extremes are more manifest than in Acapulco. Some are breathtakingly beautiful, others heart-rendingly sad.

Along the main highway, hugging the coast, and in the city itself are hotels of absolute splendour. Restaurants seem to float in shining pools of crystalline water. Swimmers drift lazily between banks of lush, multi-coloured flowers. Yet, a few streets away, in the narrow-stacked buildings of the town, seemingly just across the road, women can be seen collecting water in plastic buckets from a communal tap. Others, even less fortunate, pick through discarded vegetables at the end of a market day, looking for something fit to eat.

This is true of every city, but in Acapulco it touched me more. Two strips of humanity, poles apart in wealth and values, side by side, almost holding hands yet seldom touching. Ignored on the one hand, wondered at on the other.

Further away, one hundred and fifty miles up the coast, still in the state of Guerrero, is the tourist resort of Ixtapa. It is a newer playground, but the toys are much the same. And, unlike in some other places, crocodiles are visible in the nearby lagoons.

Much farther north, in *Jalisco* state, is Puerto Vallarta, also new in tourist terms, although the American film director John Huston was active there in 1964 when he made 'Night of the Iguana' with Richard Burton, Deborah Kerr and Ava Gardner. So were the French. They occupied Jalisco during the Wars of Intervention. These were conducted in the mid-nineteenth century by a joint force from Spain, France and Great Britain in an effort to gain compensation for debts owed by Mexico.

After the War of Reform – Mexico's history is punctuated by illustrious sounding battles – the country was financially exhausted. The war had brought to power Benito Juárez, Mexico's one and only Indian president, but it had left the coffers empty. Juárez informed all foreign creditors that

28. *Before the arrival of the Spaniards, the country was populated by many tribes, a few of which became dominant. Tribal differences have persisted to this day. Ten major Indian language groups survive, and even among these there are different dialects. These women and children belong to one such group, the Huichol Indians.*

there would have to be a two-year moratorium on repayments.

No one, outside Mexico, liked the idea very much.

The Americans tried to buy Baja California, Sonora and Chihuahua states, but the deal was rejected. They did, however, achieve a perpetual right of way across the Isthmus of Tehuantepec, the narrowest part of the neck of Mexico between the Gulf and the Pacific.

Spain, France and Great Britain, on the other hand, got out their implements and, in 1861, signed an agreement to despatch a joint force against Mexico. This landed in Veracruz early the following year. In a later section we will look at this in greater detail, but as far as the state of Jalisco is concerned, it fell to the French in the 1860s. In 1866 it was regained by the Mexicans. The following year the Hapsburg Archduke Ferdinand Maximilian, Emperor of Mexico, given his position mainly by the French, was taken out and shot on the orders of Benito Juárez, who began it all by putting off a debt and who ended part of it with a firing squad.

Before we leave the Pacific coast, let us take a look at Colima and Michoacán – and a little of the state of Puebla – and some of the volcanoes that have been active there.

Colima, one of the smallest of the Mexican states, is roughly triangular, with its base along the coast. In 1941, the volcano also named Colima erupted here, causing great loss of life. Mexico is a land of almost constant vulcanism, both literal and metaphoric. The Mexicans themselves have been called the sons of the shaking earth.

Michoacán, a much larger state lying between Colima, Jalisco and Guerrero, is one of the most beautiful in the whole of Mexico. Driving along its mountain highways, one can see the land falling away to the sea in layer after layer of greys and blues and the softest violets.

In Michoacán, in 1943, in the middle of a maize field, Paricutín, a new volcano, came into being. It is said that a farmer, thinking someone had left a fire burning among his crops, tried to stamp it out, but soon realised he had greater forces to deal with and beat a hasty retreat. So did many others. The village of San Juan de las Colchas disappeared beneath an avalanche of lava. Volcanic activity was vigorous for several months, building a cone that stands high above the surrounding landscape. At the moment Paricutín is dormant, but with a volcano one never knows. Perhaps in the near or distant future it will wake, growl and shake its fiery head.

Another sleeper is the volcano Ixtacíhuatl – pronounced Ish-ta-see-wattle – the Sleeping Lady, who lies draped in perpetual snow beside her lover, the tall, peaked warrior represented by the volcano Popocatépetl. They are not in Michoacán but stand guard on the mountainous divide that separates the Valley of Mexico from the Valley of *Puebla* in the central highlands.

According to ancient legend, they were fleeing lovers, seeking somewhere to marry and live in peace. During their flight Ixtacíhuatl became weary and lay down to sleep. Popacatépetl, after covering her with his cape, sat beside her. Both froze in the night and remain there, to this day, in their positions of surrender. In Náhuatl, the Indian tongue of the original legend, Popocatépetl means Smoking Mountain and, from time to time, down the centuries, a plume of smoke has been sighted coming from its almost-perfect conical peak. The last time was in 1928.

Popocatépetl growled and thundered when Cortés and his men entered the Valley of Mexico on their way to plunder the city ruled by Montezuma, the Aztec king. Alarmed, but undeterred, they pressed on, and the mountain fell silent. It was silent also when Cuauhtemoc, Montezuma's nephew, last of the Aztec emperors, was captured by the Spaniards, who treated him

with courtesy and respect until they found out how small his treasure was. Believing there was more stashed away, they then tortured him to reveal the hiding place, but in vain, for there was, in fact, little gold.

As the last stop on this brief tour of Mexican states we will take a look at *Guanajuato* – interesting because of what is beneath, as well as what is above, the surface of the earth. Guanajuato is a roughly circular state, some twelve thousand square miles in size, in the heart of the central highland. About two hundred miles by road separates its capital from the centre of Mexico City.

It was in Guanajuato, in the little town of Dolores, that a parish priest named Miguel Hidalgo rang the bell of his church on September 16, 1810 and called for liberty, freedom from Spain. And sparked the War of Independence.

It was from deep in the earth of Guanajuato that the Spanish conquerors extracted ton upon ton of silver and shipped it back to Spain, or used it to purchase silks and spices which, in turn, were shipped back to Spain. According to the records, in the second half of the eighteenth century Guanajuato was the principal source of silver in the whole of Mexico.

Yet the Indians who brought the silver to the surface were treated with such harshness that their numbers became decimated. When they were needed for a labour force, they were often arrested and pressed into service. In the town of Guanajuato they were not allowed to wear the traditional Indian dress of loose, white, cotton trousers beneath their shirts. For the time they spent in the city, they were obliged to hire a pair of European trousers – from the Spaniards, of course. The only surprising thing about the ringing of the Liberty Bell is that it didn't occur earlier. Or that Hidalgo's cry, *'El Grito!'* did not resound sooner throughout the land.

Today, beneath the streets of the city, are catacombs where mummified corpses, preserved by salts contained in the soil in which they were buried, grin at onlookers from their glass cases: present, but silent, witnesses to a thousand untold histories. History, after all, belongs to him who has the voice – and the wherewithal to make it heard.

Guanajuato is today one of Mexico's central granaries. From here and from neighbouring farming states such as Michoacán, Puebla, San Luis Potosí and the state of Mexico, food pours daily into Mexico City to feed the millions concentrated there. New products of the earth, new, that is, to Old Mexico, like wheat, rice and chickpeas, are consumed by the ton. Balancing these are items that were unknown in Europe until they were discovered in Latin America: potatoes, maize (Indian corn), tomatoes and chocolate. Henry VIII, for all his gargantuan appetite, never bit into a roast potato or enjoyed the fresh taste of tomato. Tomatoes were known in Europe as early as 1544, but served only for decoration – their fruit was thought to be poisonous.

The Heartland

The state of Mexico, and its core the Federal District, is the motor of the vast machine. Although small in area, some eight thousand square miles, this highland block comprising only one per cent of the total land mass holds twenty-five per cent of the population. And it is growing. Recent efforts to reduce the numbers flowing into the capital have succeeded to an extent. It is claimed that Mexico City's population growth has fallen from seven to three per cent, but even so it is still the most densely populated, overcrowded, heavily-polluted city in the world.

Mexico City overlaps, today, into the state of Mexico. There is an artificial boundary separating the D.F. (the Federal District) to define a government centre, but in reality the whole Valley of Mexico is one great sprawling suburb. Toluca is the state capital, but it and Mexico City are virtually a single conurbation.

Mexico City throbs. There is an electricity that seems to vibrate in the air. The mass of people, the mountains of food in the markets, the busses so overcrowded youths hang from them like ruffled feathers, the human sounds – talking, shouting, crying, pleading, and the ever-present wail, nearby or far off, of police-car sirens, all give Mexico City a pulsing life that is difficult to encounter anywhere else in the entire world.

But this great city also has oases of calm beauty: its many flower markets, its museums, and its remarkable colonial architecture. The overriding impresssion, though, is of noise and bustle.

If you stop at traffic lights, a group of window-washers is likely to descend on your car, attempting to earn something in the few moments you are there. In Mexico City there are not only window-washers in waiting, but vendors of all kinds. You can buy just about any accessory for your car, from rubber mats to radio aerials; you can buy chewing-gum, cigarettes, matches and cheap cigars; there are toys for the children, maps and lottery tickets, live animals such as rabbits, and, toward evening, some of the most delicate gardenias you are ever likely to see. Wherever traffic is forced to halt, there are traders who spend their working lives by the side of the road.

The huge bio-mass that is Mexico City spreads as far as the eye can see through the grey-amber haze of smog. It goes down beneath the asphalted surface, through the layers of past living beneath your feet. Mexico City was built on the ruins of Tenochtitlán, the city of the Aztecs, who were also known as Mexica – hence the present name of the city and the state. Down below, especially in the centre of the city, in the vast square known as the Zocalo where the National Palace stands, are the ruins of the massive Aztec temple called the Templo Mayor. There were causeways leading from the lake-city to the shore, and canals into which fleeing Spanish soldiers fell and drowned, weighted down by the gold that filled their pockets. Much of what remains of this ancient heart of empire is now being restored.

The National Palace, seat of presidential authority, the centre of city government, is the home of the massive Diego Rivera murals that present a brilliant, if somewhat less than clear-eyed, view of Mexico's turbulent history. In the far background rise the twin volcanoes, Popocatépetl and Ixtacíhuatl, great peaks with caps of permanent snow. Hernán Cortés marched between them when he came to capture the Aztec city. The air was clear then. In the summer, if you are lucky, you may see them from the city still, but the sight is increasingly rare.

Plan after plan has been discussed, discarded, sometimes put into effect, to control Mexico City's pollution, but with little result so far. The basic problem is that this great conurbation lies in a valley, some 7500 feet above sea level, where pollution has no avenue of escape. And the dirty air comes from dense traffic, heavy industry, and innumerable manufacturing plants, all functioning with little enforced control.

And yet the city's life miraculously expands and flourishes. The people, amazingly, considering some of their very real hardships, are colourful, sharp, infectious – in the very best sense of the word. In the Plaza Garibaldi, mariachi bands produce their lively strains, a mixture of strings and the hard, bright notes of trumpets. The name derives from the French *mariage*, and is said to have been one of the doomed Emperor Maximilian's contributions. They are there for hire, for anyone who wants music at a party, or for an erring husband crawling home at dawn to placate an irate wife, or to play the *mañanitas* on birthdays and special occasions.

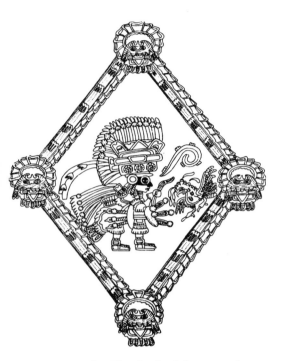

Teotihuacán: The lord of the curved knife.

Other colours, other sounds: the floral wonderland of Xochimilco, where the gardens established by the Aztecs to provide them with produce have turned into a series of walks and waterways. On Sundays, holidays, high-days, the straight canals are filled with flower-covered boats, floating bouquets in yellows, reds, whites and blues. They are also for hire. Mariachi music, voices, sounds of laughter, fill the air as Mexicans and tourists take picnics on the water. Below the boats, the canal waters are a dark and sombre green. Anything dropped disappears without a trace.

There are markets in Xochimilco – pronounced Sochi-milko – that sell fruits and vegetables, flowers and potted plants, some the height of houses; food stalls with tortillas, empanadillas, tacos and other crisp-fried foods, roasted and barbecued meats.

There are bird vendors offering bright-eyed creatures in tiny cages. Other birds, with selective beaks, will pick out a card that tells your fortune. There is a lot of Mexico in Xochimilco.

And there is all of Mexico around the city of Mexico. Those who have come to the heartland have brought their talents with them. In a sidewalk restaurant in the Zona Rosa, the Pink Zone, so called, they say, because there are so many pale-faced tourists there, practically everything is offered for sale: baskets, hats, leather wear, your portrait while you wait. There are those who make a career out of lunching in Mexico City. Businessmen, smart-suited salesmen, minor – and at times major – politicians, use restaurants as their offices, linen-covered tables as their desks. They may start at three in the afternoon and go on well into the night, hardly moving from their table. And they get a great deal done.

Around the centre of the city, like coloured beads on a coiled string, are the villages that make up the metropolis. Some are barrios with unpaved streets, their colours earthen; others sell blankets and wall-hangings; some have pottery in all shapes and designs, uses, hues and sizes. Here the colours shout with the same combination of Catholic-formal and Indian-pagan that is so deeply stamped on the country as a whole.

Mexico is a mixture of many races – something of which its people are justly proud. Mexico has survived its conquerors, those who came to alter and take. Mexico's Indian ancestors, the first people who settled on the land, had a spirit which endured; it is stamped on their faces today. The country's history could hardly have been more bloody, could hardly have cost more lives, yet what has persisted is remarkably strong. It shows itself in what they do, the way they move and, most of all, in the way they smile. A Mexican smile can be deep or fleeting, it can turn itself into a laughing face. In spite of what many others would have you believe, I have almost always found a Mexican smile to be genuine. There is laughter in Mexican eyes.

Mexico is a layered nation, a kaleidoscope of colour and sound. Now that we have a taste of it, know something of what this loud trumpet in the seas contains, we will go back and look at how it all began.

Early Civilizations

Tepexpan the Elephant Man

In the mid-1940s the remains of a human skeleton were found near the town of Tepexpan, then a dusty little *pueblo* on the road from Mexico City to the state of Michoacán. This was not a chance discovery, for the search was set in motion after the unearthing of mammoth bones by workers digging a ditch for a hospital near the town. Bones of this size caused great excitement. Archaeologists descended on the site and detailed studies were made of the area, long considered to lie on one of the migration routes taken by man on his great journey from north to south. Because an obsidian flake that might have been a spearhead or a scraping tool was found with the mammoth bones, it was decided to call in Dr Hans Lundberg, the Canadian inventor of an electrical device which functioned as a sort of archaeological mine-detector. With this device, three potential spots were located, and excavation began. In the second location, Tepexpan Man was found, in the same geological layer as the mammoth elephant. He was estimated to be about ten thousand years old.

Tepexpan Man, and others like him, were hunters of big game. They followed the herds in groups, hunted, ate, and, more than likely, sat around a fire in the evenings talking about the ones that got away. Such hunters were not the only migrants to Mexico. There were others, perhaps in the hunters' footsteps, who lived off smaller game, but also got much of their food from seeds and wild plants. There is evidence to suggest that they lived alongside, but independent of, the hunters in many places.

Nowadays it is accepted that man came to Mexico via North America, having previously crossed the Bering Strait from Asia, at a time when Alaska and Siberia were joined. There also seems to be little doubt that this migration occurred in waves. At times the journey would have been impossible; at others, an ice-free corridor appears to have been used. Whatever his origins, early Mexican Man came down south and settled, and left a wealth of evidence of his presence.

The Miller's Tale

For a couple of thousand years Tepexpan Man and his contemporaries followed their nomadic paths, hunting and fishing throughout Mexico and other parts of Middle America. There seems to have been no shortage of game. The rivers were rich in fish and eel. Apart from the elephant, camel, bison, wild horse and deer were there for the hunting, as were rabbits and other small mammals.

Eventually, they began to settle. Remains of one of the earliest inhabited sites were discovered in 1958 in the Valley of Mexico, a region that has always been relatively overpopulated. In the town of San Vicente Chicoloapan, obsidian blades and spearheads were found, together with a number of primitive grindstones, some six to seven thousand years old. These stones are important as they indicate that Mexican Man at that time not only gathered grain but made flour to use in a cooking process. The San Vicente stones are not so different from those used today by many Indians who mill their corn in the same way as their ancient ancestors.

Possibly early Mexicans gathered wild grain and ground it to make tortillas. From there they learned to cultivate it, to rely on their early corn as a source of food throughout the year. They had put their stake into the earth, and once this had rooted, they began to build.

Like all primitive peoples, they also felt the need to produce objects that were decorative as well as functional. By the beginning of the first millennium BC, in addition to ornamented pottery they were fashioning figurines which show us what they looked like, how they dressed and lived their lives, how girls beautified themselves, how a mother held her child, a woman caressed her dog... Though the precise purpose of this art form is unclear, it has left behind a knowledge of the people that could be gained in no other way. It has kept the ancient inhabitants of Mexico vividly alive, and tells us that they had enough leisure time to sit down and create.

The Dancers of Tlatilco

Until a little over a hundred years ago, scarcely anything was known about Mexican pre-history. It was assumed that the Aztecs and the Maya – the only two cultures anyone knew anything about – were the creators of the ruins and artefacts in the whole of ancient Mexico. The Aztecs were believed to have constructed the great pyramids at Teotihuacán near Mexico City, when in fact the builders of those enormous temples had been long-gone before the Aztecs reached the Valley of Mexico.

The view that anything much south of the Valley should be stamped: Made by the Maya, was undermined when investigators began to study more closely the types of ancient pottery and, in particular, the figurines, and reached the conclusion that a greater variety of peoples must have lived and died in Mexico.

Little pottery figures, mostly less than a foot high, have been unearthed in abundance all over the Valley of Mexico. One of the most important finds of such figurines was made at Tlatilco, in a pit where clay was being dug to make bricks. Among the finest and earliest examples, dating from about 900 BC, they are mostly 'dancing' or seated female figures, some with two heads, others with two profiles sharing three eyes – the ghosts of a Picasso portrait.

And while it was the clay-diggers who uncovered these remarkable little statues, it was Diego Rivera, possibly Mexico's most famous painter – his murals decorate public buildings from governmental palaces in Mexico City to the Rockefeller Center in New York – who treasured them. In the company of other artists, he made a habit of visiting the clay pits and, for practically nothing, purchased those figurines the workmen thought worth keeping. The rest were thrown away.

As a result of Diego Rivera's interest, the Mexican National Institute of Anthropology began official excavations in 1942. Thousands of objects were recovered, burial tombs were found, and the daily life of the people of Tlatilco came to be known.

They seem to have been a happy people: they danced, they played music, they kept pet dogs. I say pet dogs because certain figurines show women caressing the animals. Yet it is recorded that dogs were also used as footwarmers and often ended up in the cooking pot.

From the figurines, daily life in the early village civilization of the Valley of Mexico has been reconstructed in considerable detail. The fact that the people were depicted with little or no clothing seems to indicate that the climate was warm for most of the year. It is believed that for ceremonial occasions the women put on flared skirts and danced to the beat of drums or the music of trumpets.

Perhaps it was on these occasions that the acrobats and contortionists performed. We have a figurine from Tlatilco of a man bent backwards into a circle, his feet on his head, resting on his chest and elbows. Perhaps it was at certain festive times of the year that women put rouge on their cheeks and nipples and carried about their necks a piece of pyrite whose reflective sur-

29. *A fine example in Tepozotlán of a Churrigueresque church, part of a monastery that houses a museum of colonial-age sacred art. High above the entrance, the Virgin welcomes all who wish to enter, especially in December, when pastorelas, morality plays based on the travels of Mexican pilgrims, are performed, accompanied by fireworks and music.*

face acted as a mirror in which they could check their make-up if the dancing became too strenuous. We know that some women bleached their hair, others dyed it red.

Judging by the number of figures, women were much admired in Tlatilcoan society, particularly the steatopygous type with small waists, prominent buttocks and heavy thighs. Emphasis on these features suggests the statuettes had some connection with fertility rites. There is a remarkable little statue of a pregnant woman squatting in the position that is adopted by many Indian women today.

As families, it appears that the people of Tlatilco lived in individual huts with branch-and-adobe walls, sometimes painted red and white. Thatch roofs dotted the landscape. Some of the best hunting grounds for archaeologists are the rubbish dumps of prehistoric settlements. From these we know that the diet of the ancient inhabitants of Mexico included deer, boar, rabbit, duck, fish and iguana. Corn was their staple food – corncobs went out with the rubbish – and squashes were also eaten – vases have been discovered with pumpkin-shaped bowls.

Burial places were usually shallow graves either under the house or very near them. The interesting thing about Tlatilcoan burials is that they indicate a belief in an after-life. Bodies were wrapped in cloth or rolled up in a straw mat. Tools, weapons, clay dishes, pots and figurines were placed beside them, useful items to accompany the deceased into another world. The skeletons of dogs have also been found, presumably interred with their masters.

This village civilization of the Valley of Mexico, exemplified by the Tlatilco culture, appears to have flourished for some four hundred years, but was gradually invaded by what might be seen as missionaries from the south. These were members of a sterner race – a race that worshipped the jaguar.

The Missionaries

30. *Descendants of the Maya who once ruled the land, Tzotzil women pass a churchyard wall, barefoot as were their ancestors. Their artefacts of clay, wood and stone have come down unmodified through time. So have some aspects of their religion, which centres on talking stones and Catholic saints. (pp. 58-59)*

31. *A distillation of centuries caught in slanting light: Tzotzil Indians bearing their modern loads in the courtyard of the village church at Chamula, Chiapas. Some of the last of the Maya, they are as fiercely protective of their place of worship as were the warrior guards in the temples of old. (pp. 60-61)*

The newcomers, who some call Olmecs, although their roots may have been more widespread than that, brought with them rubber and tobacco, and a certain magic. Many of their beliefs were deeper and darker than those of the peasant community they had come to live among. They introduced a priestly hierarchy, a pecking order in society. The shallow grave beneath the floor was replaced by a burial site that was much more elaborate – if the occupant deserved it. Some have been discovered surrounded by pyrite mirrors, jade jewelery, ornaments of bone or shell, and hundreds of earthenware pots. Others were buried with nothing to distinguish them.

Other, more sinister, practices came with the missionaries. The changes are strikingly apparent in the figurines. Instead of women dancing naked, or nearly so, playing with dogs or children, looking beautiful, they depict mainly masked men with breastplates, cloaks and hats. The figurines from Tlatilco were of relaxed, easy, well-rounded people; those after the invasion of the missionaries show angrier faces, curled-back lips. We see hunchbacks and other deformities, and many with half-bent legs and arms folded in submissive attitudes, with faces uplifted in respect, as if in the presence of someone more important in the hierarchy.

And the missionaries brought with them their worship of the jaguar. This obsession with the fleet-footed, fang-toothed lord of the jungle goes back into the coils of time in Mexico. The Maya carried it on. At the time of the missionaries in the Valley of Mexico, the image of this beast was carved

32. *The crumbling façade of the church of the Virgin of Guadalupe, Taxco. Church reversals and anti-clerical legislation have led, in many ways, to the deterioration of church property.*

33. *The chapel of Los Remedios, Cholula, with the regal peak of Popocatépetl rising in the background. When Cortés marched this way, the volcano roared and thundered, as if in protest at the invasion of the land and destruction of its shrines.*

34, 36. From the most splendidly decorated to the plain and simple, church construction in Mexico boomed through the early days of the Spanish colony. Local priests, especially in the rural areas, were often the architects, the master planners. Detailed work was in many cases left to the Indians, resulting in a fusion of the two cultures and the distinctive forms of the Mexican Baroque style.

35. The church of Nuestra Señora de Ocotlán, Tlaxcala, a masterpiece of Mexican Baroque that Sacheverell Sitwell called 'the most delicious building in the world'. The focal point of its confectioned façade is the Virgin in a frame of stars. The red, lozenge-shaped bricks of the columns are in striking contrast to the filigreed heart and the elaborate towers.

37. Soaring upward, the façade of
Mexico City's Sagrario Metropolitano
lifts the spirit to the skies. Designed by
Lorenzo Rodríguez, it was constructed
between 1749 and 1768, in the heyday of
Mexican Baroque. The highly
ornamented style is called
Churrigueresque, after the Spanish
architect José de Churriguera
(1650-1725).

38, 39. *The splendid dome of Puebla's cathedral. The interior is famous for its marble floors and statuary, including a pair said to be an English king and a Scottish queen. Puebla has some 60 churches, many of their domes covered with the glazed tiles for which the city is renowned.*

40. Indian influence, felt in much of
Mexico's Baroque architecture, is
particularly strong in the state of Puebla.
The carving in the sixteenth-century
church of Santa Maria, Tonantzintla, is
a magnificent example of the marriage of
two visionary cultures. The church itself
is one of the most beautiful in all Mexico.

41. Tlaxcala, home of the Sanctuary of
Ocotlán, also known as the church of
Nuestra Señora. Gloriously decorated
inside and out, it displays a typically
Mexican fusion of Spanish High
Baroque and Indian styles.

42. *As Catholic Baroque architecture flourished in Europe, as church design and decoration grew increasingly elaborate, its ornate beauty found itself at home in Mexico. The new temples being built in New Spain demanded an intensity and extravagance of style that the Baroque provided to the full. The example on the left is from Acatepec, Puebla.*

43, 44. *Another magnificent example of European Baroque taking root in New Spain is the church of Santo Domingo, Puebla, begun in 1596 and not completed until 1659. The artistry and labour invested in this masterpiece served as an inspiration for all subsequent churches. The bell is in the tower of the cathedral of Saltillo, the finest in northern Mexico.*

45. *A mixture of religious cultures in the small town of Amecameca. Above the simple church portal is a parade of ornate Indian figures. Amecameca lies below the twin volcanoes of Popocatépetl and Ixtacíhuatl, guardians of the gates of Mexico City.*

46 . *A Passion Play parade in Tzintzuntzan, ancient capital of the Tarascans, the pre-conquest warriors who fought with Cortés. After they were defeated by the Spaniards, they joined them against the Aztecs. Without Tarascan aid, Cortés might never have overcome Montezuma.*

47. *For generations, Mexico had an ambiguous attitude towards the Church. Until recently, public Masses were not permitted, yet when the Pope visited the country, several were performed. Though religious institutions were restrained, the Catholic Church exerted a profound and widespread social, even political, influence behind the scenes. New legislators have bowed to reality and all religious organizations have been given their legal due.*

48, 49. *The great surge of church building which started in the sixteenth century continued well into the eighteenth. This lofty cathedral stands in the port of Campeche, Yucatán. From the same period is the church of San Francisco in Acatepec, Puebla, its roof ringed with angels.*

50, 51. *Whether used for daily Mass or the high ceremony of a wedding, some Mexican churches are fiercely protected by their congregations. The one above, at Chalma, Chiapas, is particularly reserved. There are no pews. To pray, families sit or kneel in groups with rows of candles before them. Permits are needed to enter the church and photography is forbidden.*

52,53. *Until 1991, a wedding in Mexico was often celebrated twice. Because of divisions between Church and State that went back to the nineteenth century, a civil ceremony was all that was required by law. The church ceremony, desired by most brides in a Catholic country, took place at a later date. Then family and friends joined to rejoice, the priest performed the holy blessing, and, in the hearts of all, the wedding was truly celebrated.*

54. The turning point for the Catholic Church came in Mexico in 1531, when the Virgin of Guadalupe appeared on a pagan site before an Indian convert to Christianity. At the former temple of the Aztec earth goddess, Tonantzin, the Virgin caused roses to bloom from the barren soil. The Indian gathered the roses and, it is claimed, they left an imprint on his cloak, which is preserved in the Basilica of the Virgin in Mexico City.

55. Although Catholicism is the country's dominant religion, it has suffered many reverses. After the revolution there was a violent reaction against the Church. For years nuns and priests were permitted to wear their habits only during services and on church property. The harsh restriction on dress and religious education were not legally removed until 1991.

56. Once Catholicism was established in New Spain, as Mexico was then known, there seemed no limit to the grandeur of the edifices built to the glory of God. This splendid Augustinian church, with its wonderful old-world interior, is at Cuitzeo, Michoacán, on the shores of the wide and lovely lake.

57. At Easter, the suffering of Christ on the cross is re-enacted in many ceremonies. Ninety per cent of Mexicans claim to be Catholic. Though other religions evangelize in attempts to increase their flocks, they have very tiny voices that are almost without effect. (pp. 80-81)

58. *The Spaniards' moral justification for conquering the Indians was to save their heathen souls by converting them to the One True Faith. The Indians, who had always had strong religious beliefs, accepted in time the replacement of one object of worship by another. But they grafted branches of their old beliefs onto the new, producing a Christin-pagan mix that has partly survived to this day.*

59, 60. *The cross, and what it symbolized, came with the Spaniards. One of the first changes the conquistadores made, whenever they could, was to destroy the Indian temples and shrines. Then they raised crosses on the sites – an expression of the triumph of the new faith on the ruins of the old. The early cross, right, re-erected in 1871, is at a sixteenth-century church at Tepoztlán, near Mexico City.*

61. The Easter pageant is performed year after year at Ajusco, a suburb of Mexico City. Thousands gather to witness the carrying of the cross and the Crucifixion re-enacted with realism and fervour.

62, 64. In Taxco at Easter, Semana Santa, the penitent cover their heads with black hoods, flagellate themselves and carry bundles of thorns, until the blood runs down their backs.

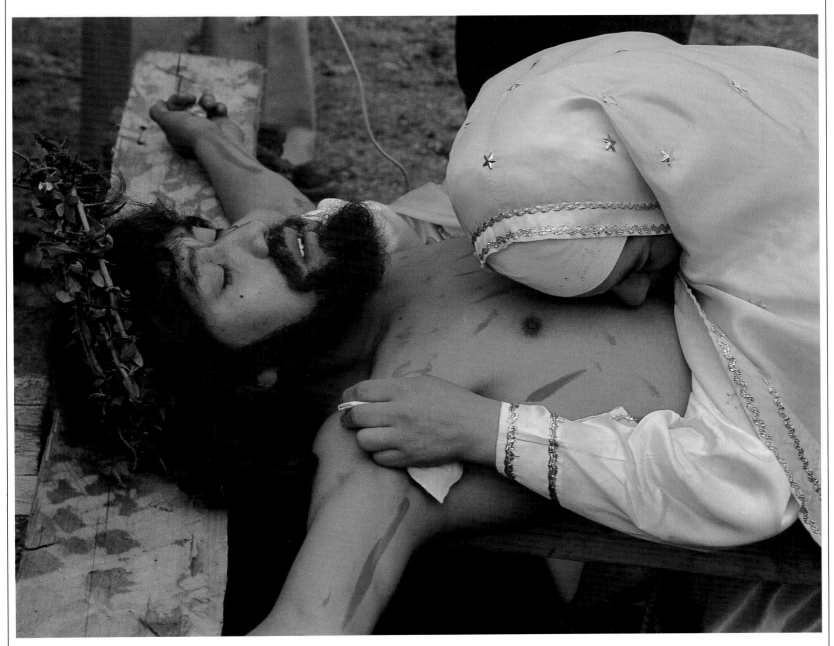

63. The participants in the Easter pageant compete for their roles and are carefully chosen. Their suffering is sometimes real. Not so very long ago a young man playing Christ died on the cross at Ajusco, possibly of suffocation. That he made the final sacrifice would have been accepted by some as fitting.

65, 66. The Day of the Dead, between
November 1 and 2, is celebrated all over
Mexico. Families gather by the graves of
the departed with offerings of food and
drink, hoping for some sign of contact –
the blowing out of a candle, the tipping
over of a glass. This fusion of old and
new religious practices is seen in much of
Mexico, for example, in the vivid Indian
murals on the ceiling of a
sixteenth-century church in Oaxaca.

67,68. *On the Day of the Dead, relatives assemble in cemeteries during the afternoon. As darkness falls, the whole burial ground becomes illuminated with the glow of candles. Incense is burned, its smoke swirling in the candle-light with the movements of the mourners. Then it is easy to imagine how the dead might actually return, if only for a moment or two.*

into ceremonial axes and altars; jaguar masks were buried with the priests; tiny jaguar masks were placed on figurines beside them.

While the early figurines of Tlatilco were made of clay, the newcomers worked with a much rarer and more precious material – jade, its hard, polished surface with shades of green, brown, almost blue, epitomizing the splendour and darker side of their civilization. The snarling, half-crouched jaguar-men statuettes are as menacing as they were in the moment of their making as they gaze with haughty and defiant eyes from the glass cases of the splendid National Museum of Anthropology in Chapultepec Park.

The new religion brought with it the cult of sacrifice, for the deities needed to be appeased with the blood of the living – or so their followers believed. The Jaguar God was a hungry god who demanded, and got, his gory dues. However, it was not all sadness and despair, blood and sacrifice, that the priests brought with them. They introduced the slash-and-burn method of cultivation, a badly needed irrigation system, and markets where produce and hand-made goods were exchanged or bartered.

Slash-and-burn farming is still practised in parts of Mexico. Forest or brush is cut back and burned where it falls, to fertilize the soil. But the benefits of this method are short-lived: after a few years, the yield falls off and fresh ground is needed. In this manner the farmers in the Valley of Mexico must have extended the cultivated areas – with their missionary landlords ministering progress.

The irrigation system, possibly the first in North America, increased crop production dramatically. Tlatilco grew from a small village to an extensive town. Markets became a regular feature of daily life. Gourds, baskets, animal skins and wooden platters were offered in exchange for beans or corn, fresh ducks or fish from the lake. Nowhere is there any mention of money, though there was very likely some common denominator that passed from hand to hand, as the Maya later used cocoa beans.

But times were changing in Tlatilco. Perhaps the Bob Dylans of the age sat on the benches in the little pubs we have clay models of, warning of things to come. Perhaps they smoked tobacco and drank pulque, a sweet, rank type of beer made from the sap of the maguey cactus, served in rawhide containers.

And disasters there were, from time to time. Fossil pollen counts show that there were droughts, when the great lakes in the Valley of Mexico were drying up. The volcanoes, Popacatépetl and Ixtacíhuatl, woke from their sleep. The Jaguar God had competition. A new Water God and a Fire God were worshipped.

Despite, or perhaps because of, these disasters, the missionary-priests, surrounded by their snarling, polished-jade idols, lorded over all. Their prestige grew and their influence spread. Some say that throughout the whole of Mexico the knowledge and skills they carried with them on their travels formed the basis on which all subsequent cultures were built. They are said to be the fathers of the art of writing in Mexico. It is believed that their architecture was the foundation on which the great temples were constructed.

But before we follow them, and their zeal, let us go back for a moment to where they came from, the jungles on the coast of the Gulf of Mexico, the jungles of Veracruz and Tabasco, the home of their beloved jaguar.

69. Grief is stamped on this woman's face as she keeps vigil beside her child's grave in the glow of votive candles. Not only in churches or graveyards are the dead remembered. By roadsides, where accidents have taken lives, crosses are often erected, fresh flowers laid, and watches kept.

Olmecs – the Big Heads

The Olmecs have been described as the first civilized peoples of Middle America, the first to develop a stratified society and social control, and then to spread it far and wide.

No one seems quite sure where the Olmecs came from, possibly one of the early waves of migrants from Asia, or from Atlantis. But no one who has seen the monuments they left in their homelands has any doubt about the power of their imagination.

Giant heads, the head alone resting on the ground, almost ten feet high, and weighing up to twenty tons, were carved from huge blocks of basalt brought to the site from some sixty miles away and left to stand for centuries. The feat of transporting the material there alone is equal to the task of bringing the stones to Stonehenge to form the magic circle.

Helmeted, Mongol-featured, majestic, these heads were carved on the low-lying island of La Venta in a mangrove swamp on the coast of Tabasco. They were part of a complex of temples, altars, platforms, of other statues this time complete with body. Some of the statues are of powerful men with broad shoulders and heavy arms. They look like warriors. Other figures are of taller men with noble profiles. They look like lords.

The Olmecs also left jade jaguars. Some interpretations suggest that the Olmecs believed they were descended from the jaguar, that he was not merely god but father to the race. These conclusions are based on etchings which show a jaguar physically mating with a human being, as if some Amazon-like mother took the lord of the jungle to her bosom and produced the Olmec race. It is possible they based their society on the belief.

In the swampland of La Venta today, oil wells, scaffolding, islands of off-shore rigging, now lift their gleaming torsos from the water. The men who created them swarm in endless teams, shift after shift, devoted to the task of keeping these new giants of the mangrove swamp satisfied.

Beliefs apart, and whatever the statues might represent, the Olmecs left enough architectural evidence to convince us they were civic designers who planned on a grand scale – a scale that was adopted elsewhere in Mexico, above all at Teotihuacán.

Jaguar-priest going on his knees toward a temple, detail.

Teotihuacán
City of Ghosts

On a scrubby plain, brown earth showing through tough grasses and cactus, some thirty miles from the centre of Mexico City, lie the remains of what was once a magnificent city. Here, long before the Aztecs came, when the plain was covered in forest, Teotihuacán was built.

Now it is a city of ghosts.

Even the mighty Aztecs held Teotihuacán in awe. They knew the city only as a ruin where wild animals burrowed and a few nomadic squatters dwelt, yet they believed it to be the Home of all the Gods, the place where the Sun and Moon were made.

At its zenith, about AD 500, it must have been a splendid city of enormous wealth and beauty. Wide avenues formed the city's grid, stately pyramids filled the skyline. There were huge plazas where citizens met and strolled, held their markets, perhaps danced to drums, trumpets and rattles as fires lit the night – under the eye of the stone plumed-serpents.

Each detail of the city seems to have been carefully planned. In the religious centres the pieces match. The themes that adorn the pyramids – the serpents' heads with their plumes, the repeated circular, all-seeing eye, the tiered stairways – are all of a piece.

There were suburbs as well, where craftsmen and labourers lived; streets and plazas were paved with loving care; there was a drainage system; some of the walls were painted. It is little wonder that the Aztecs viewed Teotihuacán as a place of wonder.

And what they saw must have been even more impressive than what we have today, though a great deal of reconstruction work has been carried out in the past fifty years in an attempt to restore to the city some of its former majesty. Not all of it has been well judged and executed. One of the pioneer archaeologists thought that the mighty Pyramid of the Sun was in too poor a state of decay to restore. He believed, however, that beneath the ruin lay another temple in good condition, so he had the outer skin stripped away to reveal the structure underneath. It turned out to be an earthen pyramid, not substantial enough to withstand the torrential rains – this happened to be the time of year when the Valley of Mexico has huge downpours, usually in the afternoon. The result was that the Pyramid of the Sun was rapidly re-covered with the tons of stone that had been torn away, so that what we see now is a fairly crude reconstruction, lacking the beautiful symmetry of the original.

Much of what the Aztecs saw has been removed by tourists. The plumed-serpent's heads that jut out along the walls of the Temple of Quetzalcoatl once had bright, sparkling eyes made from obsidian, black volcanic glass. Over the years they have been gouged out by souvenir hunters, so that now the serpents stare blindly across the ruined plain.

We do not know much about the Toltecs who built what was once the gleaming city of Teotihuacán, where they came from or where they went. They left us nothing in writing, apart from a few hieroglyphics which no one understands. We do not know what language they spoke. All we are sure about is their sense of mystery, their mastery of design.

Teotihuacán, apart from the ruins that were left abandoned, was finally destroyed by raiders from the north. They came, they burned, sacked and slaughtered. Surprisingly, the inhabitants of the city seem to have done little to defend it.

Today, as you walk from the Citadel down the long, wide, straight Avenue of the Dead to the Pyramid of the Moon, passing the magnificent Pyramid of the Sun on your right and the temples and priestly residences on your left, you can only wonder at the scale and splendour of this ancient religious centre.

Ancient Empires

The Aztecs
the Sun Warriors

They came as nomads into the Valley of Mexico and were known by many names. One of the first was Chichimec, the Sons of Dogs, which is what they were called in the north, in the present state of Chihuahua, when they were living on rats and hares, wild plants and roots. That was long before they became the Sun Warriors. They were also known as the Mexica, and gave the country its name.

They came quietly and were considered inferior by the other tribes living in the luxuriant Valley. They hired themselves out as mercenaries and were sometimes called the Bow and Arrow Men. For almost a hundred years they moved from place to place in the Valley, never staying for very long, and almost always in locations that no one wanted. For a time they camped on Chapultepec Hill, where the park in the centre of Mexico City is today. They built a temple there, but had trouble with their neighbours, being accused of stealing their wives. They were given a stretch of land that was barren and full of snakes, in the hope they might perish there. But the Aztecs survived.

In a strange way they were a driven people, believing they were chosen, that they were the Children of the Sun. They were looking for their promised land – and knew how they would find it. According to their legends, when they came to the place where an eagle, with a serpent in its beak, sat on top of a cactus, they would settle and begin to build their empire. Until then they were to search.

They searched ruthlessly, hiring themselves out to whichever side looked like being the winner in the constant wars between the rival lords of the Valley of Mexico. They were savage fighters; to them the spilling of blood gave life to their god, the Sun.

When asked why they built their temples, they replied that it was to fill them with fresh hearts and blood. When asked by the same lord – later when he needed them – to assist in a local war, they made a bargain: their freedom in exchange for eight thousand prisoners. Instead of captives, the lord was given bags of their ears as bounty-hunter's tokens.

The Aztecs moved again, this time to a group of uninhabited islands in Lake Texcoco, now an almost dried-up lake bed north-east of Mexico City. When the Aztecs and other tribes filled the Valley with their numbers, it was a richer, lusher place than it is today. Only in the village of Xochimilco (pronounced Sochi-milko) can we get an idea of what it must have looked like: a labyrinth of canals and floating gardens on the lower ground, with forest-clad hills dotting the landscape, and the giant volcanoes Popocatépetl and Ixtachíhuatl watching over it all.

In their new, but still temporary territory, islands unwanted by others in the midst of a swamp, the Aztecs' indomitable spirit overcame their unpromising surroundings. In their narrow canoes they carried load after load of ducks, frogs and fish to neighbouring villages and bartered them for fruit and materials to build their temples with – wood and lime and stone. No one prevented them. They were despised as blood-obsessed warriors who lived in a God-forsaken spot called Zoquitlan – the Place of Mud.

So they persisted, believing in their god. He was called Huitzilopochtli, translated as Hummingbird on the Left Side, and his origin has curious parallels with the belief surrounding the birth of the Olmecs. This time the earth-woman was impregnated by a ball of feathers she found while cleaning the temple and placed between her breasts. Her offspring was a fully-grown warrior, armed with a sword and with the head of a serpent. Huitzilopochtli became the War God, the Hunting God and the Sun God. It was he who told the Aztecs where they would finally settle.

In the history of mankind, many religious beliefs have been based on the contact of an earth-woman with another being, spirit or god. And even before biblical times there were peoples who believed absolutely that they were the chosen ones, seeking a promised land. In the case of the Aztecs, we know so much about them because their empire was at its height when the Spaniard came. It was their city he stormed with his muskets, it was their fabled wealth that drew him to the Valley of Mexico. A prime source of our knowledge is the codices, manuscripts, volumes that were preserved by the Spaniards, overwritten with descriptions in many cases, and translated by the surviving Aztecs, passing their story on.

Finally, in the early part of the thirteenth century, the Aztecs had their promised sign: an eagle with a serpent in its beak sitting on a cactus. This eagle is the official emblem of Mexico today, appearing on the flag, coins, letters, legal documents, throughout the country.

The Aztecs' eagle was perched on another island in the Lake of Texcoco, a soggy scrap of land that was to become the Aztec heart. That it was not firm ground and had to be reached by canoe was something they turned to their advantage. They developed a system of intense cultivation they called *chinampas* by heaping beds of lake mud and plant life in layers, piling the material until it formed a rich, prolific garden. They continued to trade their produce, and the wildlife they caught, with their neighbours.

And because they were isolated on the lake – and were the masters of the canoe – they were almost untouchable. What is more, the canoe was just about the only form of transport known in ancient Mexico – apart from the backs of slaves. The wheel was unknown as a means of transport – some children's toys display wheels but it was not put into practice outside the nursery. And no one had ever seen a horse.

In fact, when the Spanish landed, their horses with them, the Maya on seeing the animal for the first time thought it was a god. On one occasion, Cortés abandoned a lame horse, which the Maya carefully installed in a hut and brought offerings of tasty meats in delicious sauces. Of course the poor animal died, but, still convinced, the Maya built a statue in the shape of a horse and continued to worship it.

The Lake City of Tenochtitlán

On their new island the Aztecs began to build their city, called Tenochtitlán. Over the next two hundred years, it was to become the greatest metropolis in the New World. When Cortés set eyes on it, he called it another Venice. The *chinampas* beds had rooted and flowered. The trees planted to stop the beds from floating away were tall and stately. Canoes glided between the gardens along broad, perfectly-aligned canals. Three giant causeways linked the island-city to the mainland.

Tenochtitlán itself was divided into four large sections. One-storey houses of white-painted adobe, with brightly-coloured curtains and awnings, lined the streets. Almost every house had its own patio or roof-garden, often filled with flowers.

In the centre of the city was the great plaza, a site occupied today by Mexico City's Zocalo. Here was the Emperor's Palace – today it is the National Palace where Mexico's President has his office. In those days Tenochtitlán housed about a million people – one twentieth of the number that live there now.

But, in spite of their progress, their taste for beauty and order, much about the Aztecs had not changed. For many years they continued to fight, as mercenaries, the battles of other war-lords in the Valley, usually with an eye on what they could gain. At times they fought to preserve their freedom, at others it was to harvest prisoners whose hearts they needed to placate their gods.

In the middle of the fifteenth century, so it is recorded, a great cold descended on the Valley of Mexico. Many houses collapsed under the weight of snow, the lake froze, wild animals came across the causeways, and vultures filled the skies. People sold their children in order to buy food.

This was interpreted as Huitzilopochtli's wrath: he was making the Aztecs suffer the agonies of hunger because he, himself, had been insufficiently fed. Not enough blood had been shed in his name, not enough hearts had been offered. So the Aztecs went to war, took prisoners by the thousand, and sacrificed them to their god. In time, of course, the famine disappeared, the seasons returned to normal, and the Aztecs were convinced that their offerings had been heeded. Mass sacrifice was continued.

In the end it was their downfall. When Hernán Cortés and his men, with their rusting breastplates and their muskets, arrived at the city of Tenochtitlán to conquer it, they were accompanied by other Indians who rebelled when they saw their chance against the feared, blood-hungry Aztecs. The Aztec fighters, the Sun Warriors, who were trained from boyhood in the art of war, would have defeated the Spaniards had it not been for the armies of Tlaxcala and Texcoco. These tribes rose against the Aztecs, not out of love for the Spaniards, but in order to survive.

Before turning to the conquest, let us examine the other great Mexican nation that shared power, albeit a diminishing one, with the Aztecs when the Spaniards came. They were the Maya, lords of the jungle, who, in the Yucatán, made first contact with the white-skinned invaders. It was the Maya, also, who in their island city of Tayasal were the last of the ancient Mexicans to be defeated by the conquerors.

The Maya Lords of Darkness and Light

Unlike the Aztec underdogs who fought to overcome, the Maya, it seems, had always been masters of all they surveyed. Their origins are obscure. They may have grown out of the decline of the Olmecs, but their recorded history recalls no fight to power – and their writings go back to AD 68, a time when Rome was decaying, Nero was fiddling, and the Maya were coming to greatness.

Their beginnings coincide with the disappearance of Olmec culture, so it is reasonable to assume that the one gave way to the other. Like the Olmecs, the Maya used what has been called the Long Count – a mathematical system with which they calculated their highly-accurate calendar and predicted the conjunction of the stars. They were obsessed with astronomy; accurate predictions brought order to their lives. A knowledge of the passing of the days meant they would know when it was time to plant and time to harvest.

For the Maya, Time was a god. Without it they were lost. They calculated the length of a year to be 365.2420 days. Our, corrected, Gregorian calendar gives us a year of 365.2425 days. They were two ten-thousandths of a day short; we are three ten thousandths of a day too long. They got closer to a true year than we did.

The Maya looked further into the heavens than most other peoples. They calculated the length of a year for the planet Venus – and were correct to within one day every six thousand years. What is more, they were aware of their error and made adjustments accordingly.

One can only hope that they were not quite as accurate in their astrological predictions. According to the Maya, the world has seen four great cycles, each of about 5,200 years. Each has ended with some disaster – fire or flood or famine. We are now nearing the end of the fifth cycle, forecast for December 24, 2011. It seems quite soon. And the way the world is going, the Maya could easily be right.

Curiously, their brilliant mathematical minds did not see quite as clearly the relationship between cause and effect when it came to ill-health. Sickness and disease were wrapped in superstition. Here, as in other Mexican cultures, priests, not doctors, were consulted. The priest would burn incense, suggest sacrifices, even throw dice to determine the cause of the condition.

Certain herbs were used as medicines. Tobacco was thought to be especially helpful and was prescribed for almost anything from snake-bite to asthma. Modern medicine might not agree. Nor would your local physician be likely to suggest many of the other Mayan remedies, such as boiled dung of the tapir, a pig-like animal related to the rhinoceros, or mashed rooster's testicles, or even a bat marinated in a local brew.

When it came to their art, however, the Maya were superb. They had a sense of colour and design unequalled in their part of the world. Only in some of the Olmec jade statuettes is there the same delicacy of touch and many believe that it was from the Olmecs that the Maya grew.

Maya painting was found mainly in their books – sadly so many of which were burned by the conquistadores. Paper was made from tree bark, which was beaten soft, then stretched, smoothed and dried, and finally rolled, ready for use, in long narrow sheets. They also painted murals, and much of their pottery was covered with patterns and figures.

Judging by these, they were short and broad, not unlike the Olmec warriors of La Venta, the island in the Tabasco swamp. Their noses were long and curved, their eyes big and heavy-lidded, their mouths full, thick-lipped. The Maya paid great attention to their heads. Before new-born infants were a week old, they had their heads bound between two flat boards, which forced the skull to grow upward, giving rise to the long, narrow foreheads so admired by their elders.

Other devices were used to tamper with nature. Often a ball of wax was dangled over the infant, fixed firmly in its crib, to encourage the child to become cross-eyed. Such a person was considered fashionable, clever, and quite likely, if male, to join the priests. The Maya tattooed their faces, at times producing heavy scarring. The process was painful, yet was dutifully carried out by certain classes. Sometimes they filed their teeth to points and capped them with precious stones or minerals such as iron pyrites.

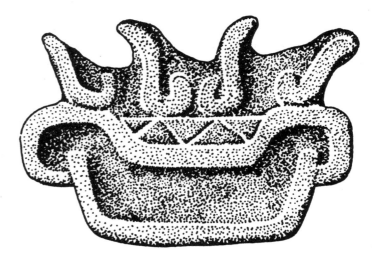

Teotihuacán: Representations of flames.

70. *In the steaming lowlands of Oaxaca a woman mixes dough, la masa, for her family's tortillas, one of the basics of Mexican life. So important is the dough that to be found 'con las manas en la masa' (with your hands in the dough) is to be caught red-handed in the act of stealing the daily bread.*

71. *High above the Pacific Coast, near the borders of Nayarit and Jalisco, live the Cora Indians. Their religious beliefs are a comingling of magic and Christianity. At Easter they paint their bodies, pray to both the Sun and the Moon, and see Venus, the morning star, as Jesus Christ. In their holy places in the mountains they consume large amounts of mescal and peyote. (pp. 98-99).*

72. *Women selling corn (maize) at a street market in Zacatecas. On other corners, in patches of shade, there will be women gossiping as they polish green avocados and peppers or purple aubergines, bright red tomatoes and chilies, to add to the carefully-arranged piles awaiting buyers. (pp. 100-101)*

73. *Anything can happen in the street in Mexico. Markets appear on a regular basis, sidewalk restaurants share space with taco-fryers who set up shop with pan and spirit stove. You can even get your hair cut by a man wearing a sombrero and a woollen chaleco in Pahuatlan, Puebla. (pp. 102-103)*

Perhaps they were dissatisfied with what their gods had given them, or, more likely, they thought deviation from the norm conferred some special power. The Olmecs, too, respected deformity, and left statuettes of hunchbacks, who were believed to possess the power of magic.

Jade was what the Maya treasured most. They had no great respect for gold. Although they wore ear-plugs, nose-plugs and, at times, lip-buttons of gold, they preferred iron pyrites – Fool's Gold is what we call it. True gold, however, was what the Spaniards wanted. In spite of their own brutality, the Maya were appalled when the Spanish soldiery cut off ear-lobes to recover an insignificant plug. Or, even more, when they sacked the Mayan cities looking for the yellow metal, often trampling valued cloaks of quetzal feathers into the ground to get it.

But perhaps the greatest contrast between knowledge and superstition, the greatest void in the mind that could calculate so accurately the movements of the stars but had no idea why a man fell ill, was the Maya obsession with self-immolation. They sacrificed captives, children, even animals, but they also sacrificed their own living bodies.

Tattooing was part of this ritual, but it went much farther than that. One of the Mayan codices that has survived shows a man and a woman drawing blood from their ears. Others, which were destroyed – and this is one of the reasons why they were burned – are recorded as illustrating a group of priests lined up in a temple. Holes were made in their penises and knotted string pulled through. On other occasions priests pierced their tongues with sharp sticks or stuck spines through their lips.

The blood gathered from such self-torture was sprinkled over the idols carved in the forms of their gods. The more painfully it was produced, the Maya believed, the more highly it would be valued.

The Mayan temples, set in their jungle fastness, were gathering points for religious ceremonies, markets, ball games and functions of the nobility. Their ruins are to be found in the mountainous area of what is now the state of Chiapas and the neighbouring countries of Guatemala and El Salvador. They are also located on the flatland of the Yucatán and the coastal forests of Tabasco.

During days of activity, families flocked in from the surrounding countryside bringing their goods to trade, to offer in honour to their lords, to place in the temples as a simple contribution to their gods. For a time the temple-city would bustle with life as lesser folk filled it with their colour and sound, pausing as a lord was carried past in a litter or a priest, his long hair matted black with the dried blood of his own offering, came among them.

When the festive days were over, the centre would be once more quiet, its silence broken by the chatter of monkeys high in the trees, the sounds of sweepers cleaning the temple precinct, or the lament of the priests in their devotions.

We have already glimpsed the majesty of Palenque, where temples and palaces formed the centre of an extended city that covered some thirty acres. Palenque was one of the first Mayan cities to be examined in detail by modern archaeologists. It has been described as the place where the Mayan architectural and sculptural genius reached its climax. In the eighteenth century it was investigated, mapped and documented, but it was not until 1952 that the most exciting discovery of all was made.

Until then the chamber on the platform at the top of the most perfect temple, set like a rectangular mansion on a truncated pyramid, had been thought of as solely for worship. But Dr Alberto Ruz, a Mexican archaeologist, looking more closely, noticed a series of holes in one of the flagstones.

74. *Silhouetted against the sky, these farm-workers are among the 2.5 million that till the state-owned land to which they have title. This ejido system, a product of the revolution, is now undergoing fundamental change. For the first time in more than seventy years, farmers will be permitted to sell or rent their land, even to foreigners. The new farm laws aim to bring capital and efficiency to an out-dated system.*

75, 76. *Etched against the cascading torrent of Agua Azul, Blue Water, this woman and her child, like the paper-maker, belong as much to the past as to the present. The high nose and fleshy lips are as Mayan as the frescoes in the fossil city of Palenque, not far from here. Progress, however, has touched them all. During the tourist season, Agua Azul can become as crowded as Mexico City.*

77. 'Death,' a famous Mexican comedian is quoted as saying, 'is so terrifying that most of us wish to become its friend.' At times death is treated lightly: candy skulls are for sale on the Day of the Dead, and children smile wryly as they bite into the marzipan. The skulls above, however, are not confections, but part of the 'recycling' system that uses graves again and again.

78. *Churches are as much the centre of the community in Mexico as in most Catholic countries. Sunday Mass is an occasion to dress up and meet friends, as well as to give praise to God. Baptisms and confirmations, weddings and funerals, are all part of the cycle of life and death that revolves around the church. Depending on the occasion, bands will lift to Heaven sounds of joy or mourning.*

79, 80. *Scenes from city life: on Sunday mornings the charros, the urban cowboys, perform in Mexico City at the Rancho Grande de la Villa, as they do in other urban centres, especially in the northern states like Durango and Chihuahua. The money they spend on themselves and their trappings keep saddlers in business and old skills alive.*

81, 82. *Scenes from country life: a rancher in Chiapas saddles his horse – for work, not display. Chiapas, mountainous and remote, still lives partly under a feudal system in which peasants and landlords each know their place. These Indian girls are drawing water from a well. Many thatched cottages in the high country of Chiapas have no running water, electricity or telephones.*

83, 84. *Mexican girls 'come out' into society on their fifteenth birthday. This is one of the three most important days in their lives. The others are their confirmation and, of course, their wedding day.*

85, 86. *A group assembled to perform the Dance of the Veijitos, the dance of the wise-ones. Masks, or substitutes for masks, like the gauze the young man wears, are an essential part of the ceremony.*

87. Masks have played an important role in Mexican ceremonies from earliest times. Priests often covered their faces. Lords and warriors wore jaguar or eagle masks as expressions of power and authority. The Maya, Aztecs and others buried their important dead with finely-wrought masks over their faces. In most markets today there are stalls with masks, usually carved wood and brightly painted, and often with hideous expressions.

88, 89. On the left, they wear the masks of the Veijitos, the little old ones, supposed to be the epitome of wisdom and experience. The bull's head, above, is not from Disneyland but from the San Domingo museum in Oaxaca. The bull, symbolizing strength and courage, was unknown before the Spaniards brought it to Mexico.

90. *Games, masks and costumes are basic to every Mexican fiesta. Music, song and dance are embraced whenever an opportunity arises. The masked dancer above is preparing to delight the crowd at Zoatecpan, state of Puebla, where she will be watched and applauded till dawn.*

91. *Fireworks are a feature of every major festive occasion. Usually elevated on a platform or a pole, they vary from the papier-maché Jadases that rain down candy in the town of Guanajuato, to this simple bull-fighter and his bull in Ayzampa, Veracruz.*

92. One of the four giant figures of the Temple of Dawn, Tula. Carved from black basalt, these atlantes are some 20 feet high and date back to about AD 1000. They once supported the roof of a massive Toltec temple, nothing of which remains except these figures.

93. *A shepherd on the road between the city of Oaxaca and Monte Albán, where the Zapotecs and later Mixtecs built their tombs and temples. He herds his flock as his forefathers might have done, wearing similar sandals, but protects himself from the mountain drizzle with a sheet of modern plastic.*

94. One of the few remaining Seri
Indians from lonely north-western
Sonora. He plays a single-stringed
instrument that emits a mournful sound,
and wears an eagle head-dress
representing a solitary high-flying bird.

95. Another reason for dressing up.
These crop harvesters in the state of
Sinaloa wear as much as possible to
protect themselves from the swarms of
midges and mosquitoes that attack them
while they work. Even so, they dress with
a sense of style – looking like summer
flowers as they go out to pick winter
greens.

96. *Think of Mexico, think of cactus, one of Nature's most durable survivors. Its form is usually rounded, to reduce evaporation, while menacing spines protect its tasty interior from animals. There are some 1500 species, from less than an inch to over 50 feet in height.*

97-100. *Cactus serves many purposes in Mexico. Tequila, mescal and pulque are fermented from its succulent heart. Young leaves are fried to give a dish called nopales. The flower fruit, tuna, is also eaten. Aloe is used for many medicines and toilet products, and from peyote comes mescaline, a powerful mind-bending drug.*

101-103. The Virgin of Guadalupe, the patron saint of Mexico, appeared to an Indian boy, Juan Diego, in 1531. The site of the visitation has been venerated ever since. On December 12, the Day of Guadalupe, thousands assemble to honour the Virgin. Dancers, dressed in traditional costume, perform ceremonial dances that go back to a time before the Spaniards came.

104-108. *Elaborate cloaks, head-dresses in the form of eagles, serpents and the glorious tail of the quetzal bird, are part of the pageant on December 12 at Mexico City's Basilica of Guadalupe. Aztecs, Maya, Toltecs, Zapotecs, all take part in traditional dress. The crowd is immense, an endless stream of people celebrating Mexico's patron saint.*

109, 110. *Funerals, burials, vigils by the grave, are solemn occasions. At times, such as the Day of the Dead, a pre-Christian element is introduced. Families spend the night by the graves of loved ones, food and drink is offered to the departed souls, and relatives wait in the hope of some sign of contact.*

111. This corner of rest, in the familiar Christian mode, is tidy and well cared for. In some areas, however, where land is at a premium, the buried one's remains are removed after seven years so that the grave site can be 'recycled'.

112. A less conventional cemetery in Chiapas, left, where the coffins, rough-planked, are left above the ground so that the spirits of the departed may more readily float free.

113-115, 119. *At times, after the rains, the whole of Mexico seems to be a flower garden. Some flowers are picked to adorn, others are dried and preserved, and a few are eaten. The prickly pear cactus-flower, known as tuna, centre, is delicious, with a slightly acid flavour similar to the tomato.*

116. *Iguanas, giant lizards that can grow to six feet in length, frequent the Yucatán. They are eaten, sold as pets, or kept chained at roadside stalls to be photographed with tourists. A pity really, as they are gentle, sluggish creatures that like nothing better than to be left in peace to bask in the sun.*

117. The black widow spider is not common, but it is highly poisonous. Only the female of the species bites!

118. Bird life in Mexico is varied and prolific. Above, wildfowl on a lake near Veracruz.

He had the stone lifted and discovered a stairwell. When the collapsed rubble was removed, Ruz was able to descend the steps to a burial chamber in which rested the remains of a Mayan lord. It was one of the most elaborate tombs ever found in the whole of Mexico.

The lord's body had been placed in a huge stone sarcophagus, elaborately carved with figures of men, animals and flowers. The lid of the coffin was over twelve feet long. When laid to rest, the Mayan lord had been covered almost entirely with jade and other precious stones. Jade plugs had studded his ears, a necklace lay in place over the bones that remained. His skull still wore a jade mask with eyes made of shell and obsidian.

He had obviously been a man of wealth and power. In fact it is believed that the sarcophagus was first laid in place and then the temple – known today as the Temple of the Cross – built above the tomb. At the entrance to the burial chamber were the skeletons of five or six young men who had been sacrificed and interred as protectors of their lord.

Sacrifice was common among the Maya, though not, it would seem, on so large a scale as among their northern neighbours, the Aztecs. The offering of live victims to the gods was the task of the priests. It was their job to tear the beating heart from the victim and smear its blood on the idol of the god being honoured. This was normally done in the chamber at the top of a temple, where the statue of the deity sat waiting for its due. The victim was spread-eagled over a convex stone, his arms and legs held by four lesser priests. Then the head priest, after dedicating the offering to the god, cut open the chest with a flint or obsidian knife – often beautifully decorated. The victim was daubed with blue, the colour of sacrifice.

Sometimes, part of the victim's body was eaten, especially if he had been a great warrior or someone renowned for his prowess. In this way, the courage of the one passed to the other. Hands and feet were considered a special delicacy.

The Maya are a mystifying peple. So much is known about them, so much has been lost. And, speaking personally, so much to be admired, so much to be condemned. My second novel about Mexico, *These Kingdoms*, which grew out of first viewing the garrisoned walls of Campeche, turned into a story about the Maya, how they lived and fought and sacrificed, now they played their deadly ball game – a game as basic as any known to man, a game of life and death.

Variations of the ball game were played by a number of Mexican nations. The Aztecs had ball courts. The Spanish conquerors were so fascinated by them they took sketches back to Europe. In fact, the rubber ball used by the Mexicans gave Europe its first contact with the material. The Maya called it *quic*.

It was the Maya who elevated the ball game to its peak. For them it was more than a duel between players, or teams of players, knocking a rubber ball from one end of a sunken court to another, the object being to gain an outright win by putting it through a carved stone ring. Like their sculptures, their bas-reliefs, the game itself became a ritual, part religious, part prestigious, certainly highly complex, in which the loser often lost his life.

Among the partly-restored ruins of the city of Chichén Itzá, in the Yucatán, the remains of seven ball courts have been discovered. One of them retains, high on one of the walls, a stone ring through which the ball had to be directed by using only the knee, elbow or hip. Points could be gained in other ways, but the ring-shot won the game.

But these were details, events by which a player won, or lost his life, insignificant beside the larger vision: the gift of their skills and talents to the glory of their gods by all who took part in the ceremony. There were no

120. Though Mexico has well over eighty million inhabitants, it has vast sparsely-populated regions where scanty rainfall and the configuration of the land make agriculture difficult, and only cacti and scrub can thrive.

holds barred in the ball game. The players wore padded leather clothing, gloves and knee-guards, chest protectors and thick belts, all of which was blessed by the priests on the eve of the game, and laid out in the court, along with fruits and other offerings, for the gods to watch over through the night. Before a big game the whole community fasted and men were not permitted to make love to their wives. It was an event that was taken solemnly.

The court was long and narrow, either sunken or built up around the sides so that spectators could look down on the game. Serpent-headed markers stood in each corner; when a point was won by gaining territory, or lost by hitting the ball out of court, counters were moved from post to post. A game, it seems, could go on for as long as the players had the strength to stand, or until the ball was knocked through the hole in the ring in the prescribed manner.

This happened so infrequently that the winner was entitled to claim the jewelry and clothing of all who watched – if they could be caught. One of the bas-relief sculptures at Chichén Itzá shows a ball player with a knife in one hand and his opponent's head in the other.

There is plenty of evidence wherever you look, and in whatever aspect of Maya culture you examine, of an amazing balance of darkness and light. One was inseparable from the other. In reaching for enlightenment, often falling back into the depths of darker superstition, always hoping their pain might lead to salvation, the Maya touched something deep within the heart of every human being. And they show us again the colours of Mexican endurance, the sun and shadow that falls across the land.

There were other great Mexican nations, tribes, peoples. We have seen the work of those who carved the mountain-top into a shrine at Monte Albán – the Zapotecs. In time they were joined by the Mixtecs, who added their decorative touches to the pyramidal tombs high above the Valley of Oaxaca.

Much further north, fifty miles north of Mexico City, the Toltecs built a vast complex of temples and palaces at Tula, in the state of Hidalgo. Two ball courts were discovered. All that remains today are the rows of giant atlantes carved in the form of warriors. On their chests are stylized butterflies, an emblem of the Toltecs.

More, many more, ancient Mexicans filled the landscape. It has been roughly but credibly calculated that before the conquest there was something in the order of twenty-five million Mexican Indians. By 1580, only sixty years later, there were an estimated three million – twenty-two million fewer through warfare and disease, through brutality and enslavement, but, above all, because of the destruction of their social order and their religion. The Spaniards took away their leaders and their gods; without them, the Indians lost their reason for living.

The Conquest
Arrival of the Horse-Gods

The first recorded Spaniard set foot in the Yucatán in 1511. His name was Valdivia and he was sailing from Panama to the island of San Domingo when his vessel sank. In a lifeboat with neither food nor sails, he drifted with several crew members to the east coast of Yucatán. There, with eleven companions, he was taken prisoner by a Maya lord and sacrificed with four others. Their bodies were eaten. The remaining Spaniards, too thin to be eaten at that time, were caged. It was not an auspicious beginning.

Later, the thin Spaniards escaped and two managed to survive. These, Aguilar and Guerrero, learned to speak Maya, married into Maya society, and were still alive when Hernán Cortés and his expedition landed at San Juan de Ullua, in Veracruz, in 1519. Aguilar became an interpreter for Cortés.

Cortés brought with him six hundred and fifty-three men, some horses, some artillery – ludicrously little to fight the Aztec nation, for that was his intention. But then, he did not know what he was up against and his belief in himself was supreme.

Cortés' adventure was inspired by greed. He was once heard to declare that Spaniards have a disease that can only be cured by gold. His belief in Mexican gold came from an earlier expedition, in 1517, when Francisco Hernández de Córdoba, sailing westward in search of slaves, landed in the Bay of Campeche. The Maya beat him off, but he reported riches because of some golden baubles he had found.

Excited by this, the following year, Juan de Grijalva, with a much larger force, followed the Campeche coast and went some way up the Tabasco River. Here, considerable treasure was gained, and the Spaniards learned of the Aztec city, Tenochtitlán, and the wealth that it contained.

In Easter Week 1519, Hernán Cortés landed and began a journey that was to alter the world. In spite of his tiny army, compared to the hundreds of thousands of Indian warriors – armed with bows and arrows, flint-tipped spears and clubs in which was imbedded razor-sharp obsidian – it took Cortés little more than two years to reach his goal. Although in his fighting force there were only thirteen musketeers and fourteen cannon, Cortés defeated not only the Aztecs who guarded the city of Tenochtitlán but several other Indian armies en route – most of whom subsequently joined him in his attack on Montezuma.

Cortés was not only a brave man, a clever leader, he was also blessed with enormous luck. Some say magic. Shortly after landing he heard of Aguilar, the undernourished Spaniard, too thin to be eaten, who had escaped to live among the Maya. Aguilar joined Cortés, although his companion, Guerrero, refused to leave his Maya wife and children.

Aguilar spoke Maya but not the language of the Aztecs, Náhuatl. This problem was solved by a gift. The gift was a woman, one of twenty presented to Cortés and his captains by the chiefs of Tabasco, the rulers of that part of the country where the Spaniards landed.

At first the Tabascoan chiefs attacked the Spaniards with a force so vast it filled the field of battle. They beat drums, blew trumpets, cried their war-cries and advanced. Cortés led his troop of cavalry into their midst. They fled. Having never seen a mounted man before, they thought the animal and its rider were one – monstrous gods that had come from the sea. The Spanish cannon had been bad enough, yet somehow understandable, Mexicans were, after all, sons of the shaking earth, but the terrifying charge of the man-animal gods was more than the Tabascoans could face. The battle was over before it began.

When the chiefs came to negotiate peace they brought gifts – among them the woman who spoke two native tongues, one Náhuatl, the other Maya. So with Aguilar as intermediary, Cortés could communicate with the Aztecs: they spoke to the woman, she to Aguilar, and he to Cortés.

The woman's original name was Malintzin. The Spaniards called her Doña Marina, the Mexicans La Malinche, the Traitress. The first is a title of honour, the second of shame. She became important to Cortés who soon took her away from her first Spanish protector and bedded her himself. She later bore him a son, one of the first of a long line of Mexicans who carry Spanish and Indian blood. To many Mexicans La Malinche is a symbol of treachery; as far as Cortés was concerned, she was invaluable.

Figurine from Teotihuacán, height 51 cm.

La Malinche, Aguilar, the horses, were all part of the good fortune that rode with Hernán Cortés. How the magic entered was through the beliefs that controlled the lives of so many ancient Mexicans.

According to Toltec lore – those Toltecs who left the warrior pillars at Tula, who were in the Valley of Mexico before the Aztecs came – the god-man Quetzalcoatl, forced to abandon Tula, vowed to return and foretold the year in which this would happen. He said it would be 1519 – the year that Cortés landed.

Quetzalcoatl was believed to be fair-skinned and bearded, as was Hernán Cortés. When Montezuma (Moctezuma, to the Mexicans) then Emperor of the Aztecs, heard of the Spanish landing he was understandably concerned. He sent gifts to Cortés and finally invited him to visit the Aztec city of Tenochtitlán.

This Cortés did, fighting a few battles along the way, gaining allies from those who, experiencing his formidable fighting ability, saw the opportunity to turn against the Aztecs and, perhaps, put an end to the wholesale slaughter of sacrificial victims demanded by the Aztec gods.

When faced by Cortés, Montezuma was impressed. There was much about the Spaniard and his weapons of death that was brutally god-like. His greed matched that of any idol. Montezuma gave Cortés a palace – and that was the beginning of the Aztec downfall.

For a time an uneasy peace reigned in Tenochtitlán. Then more Spanish ships arrived off the coast of Veracruz – Cortés had literally burned his own to make certain his men would not desert him. Cortés rushed to the coast, out-manoeuvred the new Spanish commander who had arrived to arrest him for going far beyond his original orders, enlisted the men, and returned to the Aztec capital.

But it was too late. Without his control his own force had destroyed temples, demanded food, women and gold, and the Aztecs had risen up in protest. Warriors had been massacred at a religious festival. The city was simmering. Montezuma, attempting to restore order, was stoned to death by his own people. Cortés and his men fought their way out of the city. One third died in the attempt, some at the hands of Aztec warriors, others beneath the waters of the lake on which the city was built, pulled down by the weight of the gold in their pockets.

But Hernán Cortés was not one to give up easily. He kept the loyalty of the Indians who fought with him. The city of the Aztecs was besieged. Boats were built, cannon mounted on them, the shattered Spanish fighting force reformed. Smallpox, previously unknown among the Indians, cut a swathe through Tenochtitlán.

In 1521 the Aztecs were defeated.

Maya paintings at Uaxactún.

New Spain

The Cleaning of the Slate

In the name of God, the Spaniards rode roughshod over Mexico. When Montezuma died his place was taken by Cuauhtemoc, last of the Aztec emperors. Either less convinced that Cortés represented the return of Quetzalcoatl or fanatically suicidal, Cuauhtemoc fought the invaders with bitter determination. For seventy-five days the battle lasted. In the end, the dead filled the streets of Tenochtitlán, their bodies clogged the canals, and Cuauhtemoc was captured. He asked Cortés to kill him but the Spaniard refused: he needed someone to hold what remained of the Aztec nation together while Tenochtitlán, one day to become Mexico City, was rebuilt.

In their defeat of the Aztecs, the Spaniards and their Indian allies destroyed building after building, and shovelled the rubble into the lake. When they re-built, they did so with a vengeance. Temples that had not been razed were levelled, and churches built or crosses erected on the site.

One god replaced another – with a difference: the new did not demand human sacrifice. Perhaps it was their disgust at the sight of encrusted blood on the walls of Aztec temples, the knowledge that hearts had been torn from living victims as offerings to idols, that caused the Spaniards to react with such savagery in attempting to erase the old Indian beliefs. But, react savagely they did.

Idols were shattered and thrown down temple steps, to the dismay of those forced to witness. Sacrificial chapels were scrubbed clean and images of the Virgin Mary hung on their whitewashed walls. Priests were hanged. The common people were forced to spit when the names of their gods were mentioned. Catholic priests, who came hard on the heels of the conquistadores, were harsh in their intolerance – a great part of the justification for conquering ancient Mexico was the spreading of the Word of God, the bringing into his fold of the souls of the Indians who had been denied him.

Yet, like so much that is Mexican, like so much that has happened in its history, the aftermath of the conquest was a vast shadow-play of small miracles and enormous sins.

A Spanish friar, Fray Pedro de Gante, founded a mission school to teach the Indians Spanish. He baptized hundreds of thousands of heathen souls, and when the holy water ran out, he used his own saliva. The Spanish soldiery, when brought gifts of gold in the form of richly-worked shields, beautifully-decorated discs, charming necklaces and bracelets, immediately stripped away any feathers or valueless extras, melted the gold down to ingots and hurriedly carted it away. In so doing, they destroyed priceless works of art never to be replaced.

On the other hand, no sooner had they destroyed than the Spaniards began to rebuild – not only churches but substantial houses of stone, hospitals and colleges. Mexico City was already taking shape a year after Tenochtitlán had been flattened. The fact that the new grew out of the old, that new images appeared on the walls of old shrines, gave the Indians something to believe in. Fresh seed was being planted in familiar soil in more ways than one. Wheat, olives and grape vines were introduced, sheep, cattle, and more horses arrived – the face of Mexico was changing. It was now not quite as tattooed as it had been; the colours of its differing tribes were not as clearly marked. The Spaniards made more effort than their colonial counterparts, the British, Portuguese, French or Dutch, to respect their captured territory, but to little effect.

Laws protecting the Indians were passed, some of the old tribal lords were allowed to keep a limited authority over their communities, and Aztec and Maya women married into Spanish families, but harsh conditions of labour, often no better than slavery, the destruction of society, and the ravages of disease reduced the Indian population to a shadow of what it had been.

Disease caused most of the damage. The native Mexicans had no resistance to malaria, yellow fever or smallpox. Even in areas where there was no Spanish settlement, populations were decimated: Indian travellers carried diseases with them, and insects did their deadly work. The people disappeared, animals moved in. Herds of livestock, imported by the Spaniards, took over the landscape: sheep in the high country, cattle below. Horses, mules and goats roamed where Indians had hunted or their women had grown corn.

Meanwhile, in the southern part of Mexico, in Chiapas and what is now Guatemala, outbursts of fighting continued. The Yucatán Peninsula was not finally conquered until 1546. In their initial rush toward the riches of the Aztecs, in the Valley of Mexico, the conquistadores by-passed the Yucatán. An attempt to subjugate the Maya there was made in 1527 by Francisco de Montejo, one of Cortés' captains who had been part of the Grijalva expedition, when Aztec gold had first been heard of. The initial attempt against the Maya, in spite of considerable gains, failed. So did the second which lasted from 1531 to 1535.

Only in 1546, after twenty years of sporadic warfare, were the Maya finally overcome – by Francisco de Montejo's son, a man of the same name. But that was in the Yucatán. For a further hundred and fifty years the final Maya stronghold remained intact: the city of Tayasal, secure on an island in Lake Peten Itza, in what is now Guatemala. There the Maya retained their old beliefs. Many were stamped, however, with pock-marked faces – further proof of their ability to endure. In the end, attacked by a galley built on the lake, under the withering fire of Spanish musketry, Tayasal fell, and with it the last of the Maya independencies. The work that Cortés began was over.

By this time, of course, Cortés was long dead. After Tenochtitlán, he kept the last Aztec emperor alive for as long as he needed him, then he had him hanged on the grounds that Cuauhtemoc was plotting against him. By now Cortés was suspicious of many, often with good reason. The land he had opened was rich and powerless; there were many who wanted their slice of the cake.

In 1540, at the age of fifty-five, Cortés returned to Spain, where he died seven years later, neglected by the King and his court. He was a man whom time had passed. In accordance with his final request, his body was taken back and buried in Mexico City. It remains there still.

The Years of Plunder

For the first one hundred years or so the new Spanish lords of Mexico – New Spain, it was called then – behaved like greedy children in an unattended cake shop. They grabbed whatever they could, gorged themselves, and what they could not take they often destroyed.

The first Spanish viceroy began his duties in Mexico City in 1535. One of his first tasks was to try and restrain the powers of the new landowners. These were almost without harness. Under a system called *encomienda*, a sort of land-holding in trust, selected Spaniards were given pieces of Mexico on the understanding that they would provide for and protect Indians living on their land. In return they could exact tribute, in whatever form they could lay their hands on, and labour from the natives. In effect, the Spaniards became feudal landlords, not unlike the Aztec or Maya chiefs they had so recently displaced.

Parallel with the *encomienda* system, another form of control, the *requerimiento* or requirement, was instituted. To avoid any possibility of newly-conquered Spanish lands returning to heathen habits or refusal by the natives to recognize the Pope, the *requerimiento* demanded formal submission and acceptance of the Faith. On one occasion it was read aloud, in their language, to the Chichimec Indians. However, as the reader was obliged to remain out of the range of the Chichimec arrows, he was also out of earshot. Nevertheless, the law had been upheld, the Indians had been read their rights.

This type of 'blind-eye' administration had few effective powers of restraint. The feudal *encomiendas*, with their climate of demand and brutality, contributed greatly to the decline of the Indians. They died, they disappeared. Certain men of the Church, as intolerant as they were of the idolatry they encountered, spread the teachings of Christ with great charity and patience. Bartolome de Las Casas opposed the use of force against the Indians. He believed that missionaries should go out and spread the Faith peacefully. He demonstrated this in Guatemala, where he and a group of unarmed friars converted Indians who had earlier resisted the force of Spanish arms. In the Yucatán, Diego de Landa, the first bishop there, began by furiously burning hundreds of Mayan books, to obliterate what he could of their idolatry. Then, in an amazing conversion, due perhaps to guilt once he realized what he had destroyed, became the greatest of the Maya chroniclers. He gathered what fragments remained, had those who knew them try to reconstruct the burned books and, in the end, left us a library of priceless information.

But the face of Mexico was rapidly changing. New people were replacing the old. The early years of the colony, when New Spain was more a dream than a reality, were rich – for those who were on top. At first, a dominant role was played by the chapetones, Spaniards born in Europe, but before long creole society began to emerge – a creole was someone born of Spanish parents in the new land. Mestizos, those born of mixed parentage (usually a Spanish father and an Indian mother) or children of the mestizos themselves, grew in number. Only the Indians were a dying race. New layers were seen in Mexican society. Mayan lords, chieftains and priests were replaced; only the slaves remained.

And for the creoles, with their wealth and space and time, life was rich and heady. They were living in a paradise. They could do whatever they chose. They were served by Indian hands. They amused themselves with glittering balls and bullfights, with hunting and the breeding of fine horses. Mexico City, named after the Mexicas, was clean and bright and open. Even captured English pirates, no friends of the Spaniard, were amazed by what they saw there.

In the countryside the pace of change was slower, but no less distinct. If gold had been the conquistadores' ideal booty – just melt it down and cart it away – silver was soon to replace it. Whereas gold supplies were limited, the earth seemed full of silver. In the group of states north of Mexico City, Guanajuato, San Luis Potosí and Zacatecas, one great silver lode was found after another. But silver, unlike the gold shields, jewelry and other adornments, had to be mined.

At the beginning there was a seemingly endless supply of Indian labour for the task. If Indians were unwilling to work in the narrow tunnels dug into hillsides, carrying ore out on their backs – *caballiotos*, they were called, little horses – then they could be forced to. Working under appalling conditions, they were treated little better than animals.

Other Indians, with better luck or a shrewder eye, became their own masters. Some owned the strings of mules that carried silver ore from the

Teotihuacán: Sculpture of the ancient god of fire.

mines to the mills. Mules and horses and wheeled vehicles, seen for the first time in that part of the world, revolutionized Mexico. In the mines a body of Indian shift-bosses emerged; they were highly paid and well respected. In the mills Indian technicians supervised processes they knew more about than did the Spanish owners. A Mexican middle class was slowly rising.

Elsewhere the landscape was also altering. Sheep, introduced by the Spaniards, thrived. Woollen mills were built, some owned by Indians. Woollen capes became commonplace, and the Mexican serape was born. Sugar cane, another Spanish introduction, flourished along the coast, and mills to process it were set up. A huge agrarian revolution was taking place. The pre-Hispanic human population was being replaced by an animal one; cattle, sheep, goats and horses filled the countryside.

And the money flowed – mainly into Spanish hands. Some went to Spain as tribute to the Crown, but much stayed in the cities, much went toward the building of the newest of the developments, the hacienda. As the Indian population died or disappeared, and tracts of land were left abandoned, private owners took them over. They built their castles – walled, fortress-like buildings – that encompassed all. Inside the protected hacienda there were workshops, smithies, grain stores, stables and barns. Around them their herds flourished. Their families, their hired hands were possessions. They owned everything, including the land.

Whereas the *encomienda* system granted land in trust, hacienda properties were taken and held in perpetuity. Here were the new owners of the Mexican countryside. Their properties remain, today you can see them, not far from Mexico City, with their herds, their fields, their private bull-rings. The owners wear the same silver spurs, the same type of sombrero, as their forefathers.

Hacienda power was such, its control of agricultural produce so important, that the Administration in Mexico City did nothing to prevent its appropriation of the land. No viceroy really dared challenge it. And for those who lived in their lavish comfort, with their servants, their sport and their dancing, it appeared as if the dream might never end. But end it did. Once more the Mexican winds of change were blowing strong across the landscape.

Not only was the Indian labour force being ground almost out of existence, but the creoles, the new Spaniards of the land, were beginning to raise their voices against that of Spain. They resented being treated like dumb colonial cousins. They resented the fact that administrative posts were given to Spaniards sent from Spain – often men who were there for the job in hand, soon to return, who had no future in the country. And who saw the creoles as vain and overblown, overdressed and greedy.

What is more, the powers of the creoles were being increasingly restricted. King Charles I of Spain (1516-1556) outlawed slavery. Though not, it would seem, primarily for humanitarian reasons. Slavery for Spain had been a pretty good business: the entire population of the Canary Islands had been sold as a job-lot. What concerned the Spanish King was the amount of power in colonial hands. He saw the New Spain drifting away from the Old, and with it the wealth he had come to rely on to finance his European wars. From the twin ports of Veracruz and Acapulco, one on the east, one on the west, gold and silver flowed to pay for the needs of Spain, each convoy escorted by armed galleons to fend off the pirates who swarmed the seas like sharks.

To protect his interests, the Spanish King abolished free trade. Royal officials monitored ships arriving in Spain at the ports of Cadiz and Seville. Nothing produced in New Spain was allowed to compete with goods in the

122. *A wayside picnic, a common sight on Sundays or holidays. Whole families camp beside the highway, prepare tortillas, sip a bottle of fizzy pop, and snooze away the afternoon. It is a pleasant moment of escape for many who live in crowded Mexico City.*

123. A fast-food distribution centre, Mexican style. In a corner of a marketplace a woman waits with hot tamales – spiced corn paste, fried and wrapped in corn leaves – to eat as you admire the handicrafts or bargain over items on the parades of stalls.

124. Mexican hands still produce a distinctive range of artefacts that have their roots in a native past. On display at markets all over the country, these handicraft products continue a fashion that has come down through the ages almost unaltered by time.

125. Food stalls outside the church of San Francisco in Tlaxcala, site of the oldest surviving church in Mexico. With its façade of red tiles and majestic interior, this is one of the most beautiful churches in the country.

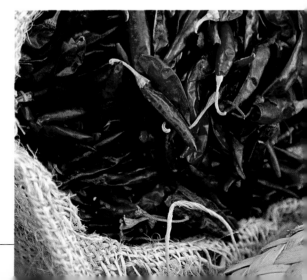

126-133. Mexican edibles, distinctive, curious, often hot, mostly wonderfully tasty, range from the very sweet, like the tiered cakes or pancakes with sunflower seeds, top right, to spicy chilies. In between are guacamole sauces, made from avocados and onions, exotic things like fried cactus grubs, centre top, pork crackling, or even iguana in green tomato or chocolate sauce.

134-138. Above, a typical spread, the table groaning with rich and varied food and drink. A selection of grilled meats, served with spring onions, may be accompanied by green tomato sauce, made with onions, coriander and chili. A starter could be corn soup with chopped pork and herbs. Corn also comes as huitlacoche, when the cob is invaded by black fungus that lends a wonderfully smooth, mushroom flavour. And, of course, there is the ubiquitous tortilla, part of every meal.

139, 140. A glittering range of chilies is available to the Mexican housewife. Pulque, made from fermented cactus, is there for the asking. 'A tortilla, a jug of pulque and thou beside me in the cactus,' might have been proposed by some distant Mexican Omar Khayyam. On the other hand, it might be more comfortable in one of the thousands of restaurants with which the country abounds.

141. *Chicharrón, crackling deep-fried pig skin, another delicacy. Served with refried beans, scrambled eggs, a splash of green tomato sauce, and then wrapped in a steaming-hot tortilla, it goes down very well with an ice-cold glass of excellent Mexican beer.*

142. A market place in Pátzcuaro, where both fresh and dried fish from the lake are on sale.

143. Pátzcuaro, where Tarascan Indians cast nets shaped like dragon-flies to catch the lake's delicately flavoured whitefish, which pollution is unfortunately making scarcer. Tarascans, who have their own native tongue, have lived by the lake for a thousand years.

144. The large Tarascan dug-outs that glide across the waters of the lake are used for fishing, transporting goods, and carrying people from the steep green islands to the shore. Nowadays, many Tarascans prefer to take the ferry when they come to town on market day.

145, 146. *Agriculture is undergoing a process of steady reform. New laws have given much needed greater freedom to the farmers, especially those who grow corn (maize), the country's staple grain. These coffee growers in the state of Chiapas should also benefit from what is called Mexico's second agrarian revolution.*

147. *Endless rows of beans curve away into the distance as these harvesters take lunch on the fertile plain of the Gómez River in the rich agricultural area near León.*

148-150. In Mexico, you can eat outdoors in all kinds of places: on boulevards, in alleys, on the corner by the traffic lights. The choice ranges from expensive sidewalk bistros to one-woman operations.

151. Preparing pulque, a sweet, thick liquor said to have been drunk by the Aztecs, requires that fermentation takes place in animal hides. These sheep skins may be used for such a purpose.

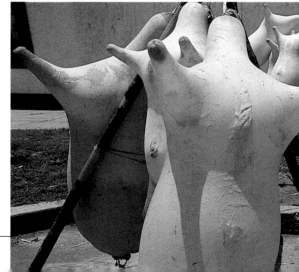

152, 153. The tortilla, made from corn (maize) flour, is, without a doubt, Mexico's daily bread. The unleavened dough is patted flat and rounded, then baked on a griddle. It can be filled and rolled up to make a taco, filled and fried to produce an enchillada, a quesadilla, a tostada, or any of the other delicious variants.

mother country. Imports of wool and silk, wine and olive oil, were restricted or prohibited. All economic decisions for the colony were made by the mother country.

The creoles seethed.

Out of their discontent the first flame of rebellion flickered. Martin Cortés, son of the conqueror, half-brother to the boy born to La Malinche, arrived in 1563 with dreams of walking in the footsteps of his father. He was, however, a lesser man. But he boasted – and conspiracy began. With two brothers named Avila he gathered a band about him with plans to separate New Spain from Europe, in the interest of the creole landowners. The Audiencia Council, the power behind the viceroy's throne, turned on them savagely. The Avila brothers were beheaded. Cortés was luckier. He was finally sent back to Spain, where he survived with no further links with the colony.

The Audiencia came down heavily on any others they suspected of being involved in the plot. Many were arrested and tortured, some were executed. The ferocity was such that for two hundred years the creoles put aside any serious thoughts of rebellion. They went back to their bull-fights, cock-fights, glittering balls, as substitute for political excitement.

Some, however, were faced with serious problems of a very different nature: Mexico City was sinking.

When the Aztecs found their promised land, where the eagle settled on the cactus, it was an island in a lake. There they began their city and surrounded it with *chinampas*, piles of mud and plant life, which in time became a little firmer and were built on. To keep water away from the city during the downpours from June to September, the Aztecs had a system of dykes. The Spaniards neglected these, and most of them crumbled. So when the rains came down, especially in the early part of the seventeenth century, serious flooding occurred, the lake level rose, and the Aztecs' original island became known as the Isle of Dogs – that is where the poor animals fled to.

What made matters worse was the amount of tree-cutting the Spaniards had indulged in. The bare hills that surround Mexico City today were once covered with forest, most of which was felled for building, making it easier for rainwater to run down the hillsides into the lake. And into this wet, unconsolidated ground Mexico City was sinking. The new colonial houses, built of stone, were disappearing rapidly.

This was a process that has never really stopped. The beautifully domed Bellas Artes building in the heart of modern Mexico City has had tons of cement injected into its foundations to prevent it sinking further. Other older structures can be seen to have a decided tilt.

The first real attempt to deal with the floodwaters was made in 1604. A tunnel, four miles long, was bored through the mountains in the north-west of the Valley. Indians by the thousand were forced to dig, often waist-deep in mud. Hundreds of them died. The tunnel, completed in less than a year, proved to be a total failure: its walls collapsed almost immediately, and the mouth became choked with debris. For more than twenty years teams of Indian workers were kept at the tasks of cleaning, clearing, rebuilding – all to little effect.

In 1629, after months of rain, the city was flooded once again – this time it seemed to be permanent. For four years several feet of water kept the city dislocated, unable to function normally. The Isle of Dogs gave refuge to more than fleeing canines. Many residents moved to firmer, higher ground as their houses collapsed into the muddy waters. Canoes were used for transport, a sight that would have gladdened an Aztec's heart.

154. A woman from Oaxaca prepares a tortilla in the ancient manner, using a type of kneading stone. Terracotta figurines from Jaina, a thousand years old, show tortillas being made in exactly the same way on an identical stone, the metate, known throughout Latin America.

When the floodwaters did recede, thanks mainly to a series of less rainy years, a bolder decision was made. The clogged tunnel through the mountains was to be turned into a valley, a wide, open channel that would keep Mexico City dry. It took ten years to dig. Thirteen miles of gulch were carved out, and even then the job was incomplete – but it worked. Until the end of the eighteenth century further extensions to the Tajo de Nochistongo, as it was called, continued. And although, today, Mexico City is drier than it was and the newer buildings are more securely based, floodwaters still cause death and damage. Whenever there are very heavy rains, underpasses in the city's main arteries fill, and in the newer, crowded, frail suburbs that cram the hillsides rain turns the unpaved roadways into tracts of mud.

But at the end of the seventeenth century Mexico City seemed, once again, to be the promised land. For another hundred years life continued at a blessed pace, largely untouched by the events that rocked Europe or affected the Spanish Crown. The assumption of the Spanish throne by the Bourbons, replacing the Hapsburg monarchy, had no echoes in Mexico. The War of Spanish Succession was over the horizon, many thousands of miles away. It was not until the American colonies obtained their freedom from the British Crown in 1781, and the French rose up in revolution in 1789, that the seeds of Mexican independence began to show above the soil. Mexican creoles realized it was time to leave the motherland. Spanish sea-links had been broken. Britannia ruled the waves. Spain was allied with France. And the Spaniard had, in a sense, become another foreigner as far as the creoles were concerned.

When, in 1808, Napoleon sent troops into Spain and the Spanish people rose up in protest, the divisions in the motherland had far-reaching repercussions. The creoles in Mexico were uncertain where their future lay. One viceroy was arrested, another arrived. The shouts of independence grew stronger day by day.

The Break with Spain

The first flowers of independence showed their faces to the sun on September 16, 1810. On that day Father Miguel Hidalgo y Costilla rang the bell of his church and called on his parishioners to rebel. For some time he had been plotting with a group of creoles to launch an uprising against the Spanish rulers in December, but their scheme was discovered. Informed that the military authorities were about to move against them, a young creole officer rode through the night with a warning, and Hidalgo rang his bell.

His parishioners responded. Together with another creole officer, Ignacio de Allende, Hidalgo led his followers from his dusty town of Dolores, in Guanajuato, to San Miguel, where the Spaniards surrendered. Today, San Miguel de Allende, as it was henceforth called, is a pretty, old-style colonial town with, seemingly, more American than Mexican residents, many of them writers, painters, craft-folk.

At the outset, the uprising was largely peaceful. There was some rioting in San Miguel, but nothing like what lay ahead. When Hidalgo turned his followers, numbering some fifty thousand, to the city of Guanajuato, the mood was that of a peasant revolt. Alongside their colourful banners, darkness rode the landscape.

The city of Guanajuato was rich. Ton upon ton of silver had brought it unmeasured wealth. Hidalgo's followers were, in the main, poor Indians. The two sides were not destined to mix. Not peacefully. Not without the shedding of blood.

Fray Antonio Tello.

When the Spanish commandant of Guanajuato heard of the uprising he moved his forces into a large, massive-walled granary at the bottom of the town. Into this fortress he put the Spanish inhabitants with all their gold and silver. It was a mint, a treasure-trove waiting to be sacked. And sacked it was.

Hidalgo called on the Alhóndiga de Granaditas, as the granary was known, to surrender. It refused. The army of Indians and mestizos, with its sprinkling of creole army men, attacked. Fire poured in and out of the Alhóndiga. Many died, among them the commandant of the Spanish forces. In the confusion a group of Hidalgo's attackers, using flagstones to protect themselves from rifle fire, managed to get close enough to the wooden doors of the Alhóndiga to set them alight.

It was the end of all those sheltering in the granary. Those who did not die that day were shot later when a Spanish force arrived to avenge the town. By now Hidalgo's insurgents were little more than an undisciplined mass of peasants and creole soldiers. His famous cry for freedom from Spain – *El Grito* as it came to be known, a rallying cry against all shackles, when the mayhem had been forgotten – was now a yell for plunder as well as independence.

From Guanajuato the army moved south toward Mexico City, taking over villages as they went. Years of service in the mines, appalling conditions underground, seeing wealth torn from the countryside to go to soft Spanish hands untouched by toil, had nourished a deep-seated, bitter envy. Now it was breaking loose. Peasants who had been treated like slaves by landowners shared the same furious sentiment. They took what they could and killed any who stood in their way.

Other northern towns, those who had been branded by the same iron, endorsed the revolution. It was a class struggle now. Independence from Spain was not the only force that drove it. Mexico City lay ahead. It held shapes enough to give reality to all their feverish dreams.

In the pine-covered mountains on the western rim of the Valley of Mexico, Hildago's force was met by units of the Spanish army. Seven thousand soldiers faced eighty thousand insurgents. A fierce but inconclusive battle ensued. Eventually, the trained soldiers retreated in some order, but left open the downward path to the richest prize of all, Mexico City.

Then, some say, a miracle occurred. Hidalgo turned his forces around, and they straggled away from the Valley, many back toward their homes. No one is sure why Hildago retreated, why he left Mexico City untouched. Perhaps he had had enough of blood and slaughter and knew what would happen if his army ran wild in the city. Perhaps the fire within his tall frame, with its gaunt face and burning eyes, had died.

Whatever the reason, it was the end of Hidalgo as a real leader, though his cry, *El Grito*, rang on.

He was captured finally, as was his co-leader Ignacio de Allende. Both were shot. Hidalgo suffered the ultimate indignity from the Church: he was defrocked, excommunicated, before he was handed over to the military for execution.

But what Hidalgo began did not die with him. Too many years of suffering lay unaccounted for, too much hatred of all who ruled remained unerased. Another priest took up the banner. He was José María Morelos, a much more practical man. Where Hidalgo had led an unruly mass, Morelos organized bands of fighters. Whereas Hidalgo had been a creole, Morelos was a mestizo, a true Mexican son of the soil. And while Hidalgo had marched through the open, hilly country of Guanajuato, Morelos held strong in the almost impenetrable hills above Acapulco. With him was

Vicente Guerrero, an able fighter, after whom the state was given its present name.

For four more years Morelos and his men continued their hit-and-run offensive against the Spanish army, led by another formidable commander, General Felix Maria Calleja. Calleja was later to become viceroy, his opponent, Vicente Guerrero, one of the Mexican Republic's first presidents. There were many honours waiting to be gained in the bloody years of struggle. But not for Morelos. He was caught and executed in 1815 and, for a while, it was thought that the fires of rebellion had been extinguished. Only in the mountains above Acapulco did skirmishing continue – led now by Guerrero – and in the forests behind Veracruz. Other guerrilla leaders were offered peace and made it.

Yet the groundswell continued. *El Grito* was still heard, however faintly. However, when independence came to Mexico it came with less than a bang and more of a whimper.

In 1820, when Spain was once again free of the French, and adopted a much more liberal attitude toward its colonies, a constitution was offered which would have included a representative government in Mexico, albeit tied to the Spanish Crown, and a form of democracy that would have given most citizens the right to vote.

While the creoles in Mexico welcomed a chance to run their country under the guise of a parliament, they abhorred the idea of democracy. More plotting began. This time a group of church and laymen talked of a coup d'état against the viceroy. For this they needed military help and enlisted a creole officer, Agustín de Iturbide, who was currently out of favour, his crime: the demanding of monies from mine owners to see that their convoys of silver were safely delivered. Not the best of recommendations, as his fellow-plotters were later to discover.

When Iturbide was restored to grace in the army he was sent against Vicente Guerrero, to attack the insurgents' stronghold above Acapulco. There was nothing uncertain about Iturbide's ability as a military man: he had led one of the most successful attacks on José María Morelos. However, by now his ambitions went much further than mere skirmishing. He had his eye on another of the prizes to be won in this intermittent war – an imperial crown.

After a certain amount of fighting against Guerrero, Iturbide approached the rebel leader and suggested a pact which became known as the Three Guarantees. Under it Mexico was to be an independent kingdom, Catholicism would be the only recognized religion, and there were to be equal rights for all Mexicans, regardless of race. Also there was to be no interference with property, and anyone who wanted to leave Mexico could, taking their money with them.

Suddenly, after years of fighting, indecision and uncertainty, both in Spain and in Mexico, the Three Guarantees seemed to offer a solution acceptable to all. Enthusiasm spread throughout the country. Insurgent leaders and army generals stood side by side. Iturbide was triumphant. The Spanish viceroy resigned.

On September 27, 1821, Agustín de Iturbide rode through Mexico City at the head of his Trigarante Army – the Army of the Three Guarantees. There, in what is now the Avenida Madero, an arch of triumph was raised. Mexico had its freedom. Its internal troubles were about to begin.

The triumphal arch, made of wood and plaster, remained a monument for a little while, to be replaced by Mexico City's famous House of Tiles. It was made of sterner stuff and can still be seen there today. Iturbide, himself, did not last much longer.

Independence

The New Republic

When the euphoria had faded and the reality of independence faced them, those in power in Mexico City were appalled by the enormity of the task that lay ahead. Mexico had no government or parliament. It had pledged loyalty to the Spanish king, but his viceroy had no voice. There was no constitution or anything like a civil service. Many Spaniards had gone home, taking their money with them. There was no cash in the bank, the mining industry was in ruins, and there had been ten years of spluttering warfare which, although the two sides were now allied, had left a bitterness that was not to be easily shed.

As always it seems, in the aftermath of any revolution, bloodless or otherwise, there were shadows in the corners of even the grandest rooms, plotting, taking sides, giving their ambitions bright, if uncertain, shape.

Augustín de Iturbide, as head of the provisional government and regency council, as head of the Army of the Three Guarantees, had all the power he needed, but lacked the ability to put it to good use. He was aware of the plots around him – to declare a real republic or to return to Spanish rule. He took, what must have seemed to him, the simplest route. He made himself emperor, master of all.

And he stage-managed it beautifully. On the night of May 18, 1822, troops took to the streets, firing into the air, setting off sky-rockets, shouting: 'Long live Agustín the First, Emperor of Mexico.' The whole city was alight as crowds joined the military and marched down to the National Palace where Iturbide came out onto the balcony to receive their acclamation. The following day, at seven in the morning, Congress met and voted its approval. Two months later Iturbide was crowned emperor in Mexico City's cathedral. It was his moment of supreme glory. From then on it was all downhill.

The proclamation of Iturbide as emperor so soon after years of bloody struggle, the elevation to supreme power of a man of dubious character and previously subordinate to so many he now had control over, was a farce. His title meant nothing. There were those who could not mouth it without a smile.

In more practical terms, Mexico's financial mess got worse. Paper money was printed, inflation soared and, worst of all, the army was not being paid. When Congress criticized Iturbide, he reduced its number, relieving of their posts those he did not trust. The plotting continued. Over the brightness of Iturbide's imperial uniforms, the emperor's colourful new clothes, dark shadows fell.

The next Mexican whose star was to rise was Antonio López de Santa Anna, the army officer who introduced chewing gum to the United States, who overran the Alamo, and who was to go down in history for many more things besides.

Santa Anna first made his differences with Iturbide felt when he was transferred to Veracruz – presumably to keep him from meddling in the capital. He was not the sort of man to be pushed aside. Handsome, big-jawed Santa Anna was to hold the reins of power in Mexico for the next thirty-five years.

Very soon after being relocated to Veracruz – he formed an alliance with another insurgent leader, another of those from the years of turmoil who was one day to be president, another colourful Mexican who was to indulge himself in a curious name change. As rebel leader he had been known as Felix Fernandez; now he became Guadalupe Victoria, the name under which he passed into history – a little like Pancho Villa in reverse.

Santa Anna and Guadalupe Victoria declared a republic, absolutely free and removed from Spain. More fighting broke out. For a while

Iturbide's unpaid army supported him, then joined the Republicans. Deserted, floundering, Iturbide offered his abdication to Congress. It was promptly accepted, and he was immediately banished from the country for life.

Unfortunately, after leaving on the British merchant vessel *Raulins*, Iturbide did not stay away. Within a year he returned, hoping to defend his country against a Spanish attempt to reconquer Mexico. He was almost immediately captured and shot. So ended Mexico's first latter-day emperor. The second, and last, as we shall see, suffered a similar fate.

Meanwhile Santa Anna took over the running of the country. He saw to it that Guadalupe Victoria was installed as the Republic of Mexico's first president, then turned his attentions elsewhere. Things were moving on the northern border. United States farmers, cattlemen, settlers, were encroaching on Mexican territory, which included what are now the U.S. states of California and Texas.

During the second half of the seventeenth century and for most of the eighteenth, while Mexico – New Spain as it was then – was relatively free from internal strife, its northern frontier had crept steadily forward. This was due, at first, to the work of Jesuit and Franciscan missionaries taking the word of God to Indian tribes. The task had not been easy. The Chichimecas, those Sons of Dogs, forerunners of the Aztecs, now had horses, and little time for intruders.

For a long time the missionaries made slow progress. However, matters improved when new mines were opened up in the eighteenth century. New towns were founded as far north as San Francisco, which still bears its Spanish name, as do Los Angeles, San Antonio and Albuquerque.

Spanish colonization of Texas had begun in the late seventeenth century and the Texas territory, with ill-defined boundaries, was established in 1727. By the Treaty of Florida signed in 1819, the U.S.A. relinquished all claims to Texas as part of the Florida Purchase deal. Two years later, newly independent Mexico granted Stephen Austin and his followers the right to establish a foreign colony in the sparsely populated territory. In spite of their legal cover, these northern settlers were squatters, taking what was available, doing so quite freely because there was nobody there to stop them. Until General Santa Anna rode into Texas in 1836 to throw his weight into the struggle.

At first the newcomers moved in under the guise of becoming Mexican citizens, of acknowledging Mexican sovereignty to the rich and fertile plains, but the Americans spoke no Spanish, had little time for Indians, and were newly independent themselves. They wanted no foreign laws.

In a few years their numbers, including those of their black slaves, ran into the tens of thousands. The Mexican government became alarmed. In 1830 further immigration was forbidden. A customs barrier was set up along the frontier. Smuggling became a way of life.

Over the next few years the situation worsened until a Mexican force, sent to reassert authority, was defeated in San Antonio. So in the spring of 1836 along came Santa Anna. The only opposition he found was in a small mission settlement – the Alamo, a name that rings down through history. General Santa Anna defeated the Americans defending their fort under circumstances that depend on who is telling the tale. In the American version, the leader of the garrison, William Travis, the frontiersman, Davy Crockett, and the knife-wielder, Jim Bowie, all died like heroes. One Mexican account, published two months after the fall, agrees about the deaths of the first two, but describes Bowie as 'dying like a woman, hidden under a mattress'.

Sketch of the interior of the Cathedral of Guadalajara.

Santa Anna's victory, however, was short-lived. He continued his march through Texas, the Americans retreating before him until they reached Lynchburg Ferry on the San Jacinto River. Here the battle was fought that decided the fate of Texas. The Americans, led by Sam Houston, defeated the Mexicans and captured Santa Anna when he was trying to escape in civilian clothes. In return for his release, Santa Anna signed an agreement acknowledging Texas as an independent state.

It was an agreement, however, that was not as easily accepted by the Mexican government. It was unhappy with Santa Anna and he retired for a while. But before long this colourful, always-shifting man would be centre-stage again. In the years between the downfall of Iturbide and the loss of Texas, Santa Anna had cast his shadow over Mexico on more than one occasion, selecting presidents, shaping the course of history. He was soon to do so again.

The French Connection

Between the years 1824 and 1838, between the election of the first President of the Mexican Republic and until shortly after the loss of Texas, a number of presidents held office, some of them for very brief periods, some twice, but none of them was particularly successful.

They were difficult times. A new motherless country was stumbling along in the dark, heavily in debt, inadequately controlled, with little sense of direction. And it had experienced its first international conflicts. Blood had been shed, not only over Texas, but the Spaniards had returned, hoping to reconquer their lost colony.

Led to believe the task might be easy in view of the problems facing Mexico, King Ferdinand VII sent a force to reassert his authority. It landed at Tampico, in the Gulf of Mexico, in 1829. General Santa Anna rode to the rescue. After a few scuffles the Spaniards surrendered, having lost some two hundred soldiers in battle and more than three times that number to yellow fever. Santa Anna became a national hero.

155. A charro, part-time Mexican cowboy, whose pastime is to dress up superbly in his grand sombrero, his woollen cloak or jorongo, and his fine, hand-crafted boots, and ride his bloodline steed to the cheers of his companions and the sounds of a mariachi band in a splendid Mexican rodeo.

As far as other national heroes were concerned, many suffered fates that were not quite as glorious.

Guadalupe Victoria, the former insurgent leader Felix Fernandez, completed his term as president – an achievement remarkable enough in those days – but, like his new name, his term in office had been flamboyant but somewhat empty. He was replaced, with the help of Santa Anna, by another military hero Vicente Guerrero, who did not last quite as long. He, too, was what his name implied: Guerrero, warrior in Spanish, seemed lost without a rifle in his hand. He was uncomfortable with the trappings of state, uneasy among those who noticed his country manners, and poor education. After some political in-fighting, he was ousted by his vice-president, Bustamente, taken away and shot.

Bustamante held the job for another two years. He tried to restore some fiscal order, but his harsh methods were very unpopular. He was forced into exile for a while. And, who was next in line? Of course, it was Santa Anna.

Carried by a wave of popular acclaim, Santa Anna was chosen president, but, with seeming modesty, side-stepped the post. He allowed a coadjutor to run the country instead while he waited, in his luxurious hacienda, in the foothills near Veracruz, watching from a distance.

He did not have long to wait. Two years later, after a series of bizarre measures adopted by Congress, which included the releasing of monks and nuns from their vows, Santa Anna stepped in again, this time as dictator. The liberal Congress and its ideas were sent packing. No one was shot this time, and a conservative body was installed.

Once more Santa Anna returned to the comforts of his hacienda in the balmy, semi-tropical luxury of Veracruz, until events in Texas got him moving again. This time, following his capture by the Americans and the loss of Texas, he was in disgrace. Until the French came to his rescue.

The French government, also conscious of the perilous weakness of Mexico, saw an opportunity to interfere. Whatever their long-term plans were, they presented a demand for compensation for damage to French property during the political uprising in 1828, when Guerrero came to the presidency. In particular, the French referred to a cake shop. What followed became known as 'The Pastry War'.

When Mexico refused to acknowledge the claims, stating, in no uncertain terms, that they were not responsible, the French sent a fleet to Veracruz which blockaded the port, then captured the fort of San Juan de Ulua, a monument of Mexican pride.

Veracruz was close to Santa Anna's heart and hacienda. On his white horse he hurried to the rescue. In the fighting that followed the white horse was killed, the French were routed, and Santa Anna lost a leg. Although the Mexican President finally did make a settlement with the French, Santa Anna's lost leg was a turning point in his career. His bravery won him back his lost popularity. Some years later his leg was dug up in Veracruz and reburied in Mexico City amidst much pomp and circumstance. To this day his wooden leg, or one of them, complete with highly polished boot, can be seen in the Hall of Arms, in the National Museum of History, Mexico City.

Comic opera? Perhaps, but Santa Anna, for all his grandiose gestures, had one of the shrewdest minds in the history of Mexico. What is more, he was a long-term survivor, and there was not a great number in that category.

And even though the next step in his undulating career, the War with the United States, was another slip into darkness, he was to occupy the Mexican stage for many years to come.

156. Originally, the Totonac Rain Dancers searched yearly for their sacred pole. Gifts were laid by the tree the night before it was felled. Now the pole is permanently in place and the Rain Dance is a daily event. Traditionally, it was performed only on Corpus Christi, and the four men circled 13 times so that their numbers multiplied gave 52, the number of weeks in a year. (pp.162-163)

157-159. At El Tajín, near Papantla in Veracruz, a modern version of the Totonac Rain Dance is performed. In groups of five, the men climb to a frail platform and wind their ropes around the pole top. Then, flinging themselves out into the air, four descend while the fifth, with flute and drum, accompanies them as they circle slowly back to earth.

160. One man and his dog in the rugged
state of Chihuahua, once a huge exporter
of copper and cattle. The Santa Eulalia
mining camp has one of the biggest
smelting plants ever built by man. The
dog is clearly not one of the tiny breed
that took its name from the state.

161. A milkman plods his weary way
through the streets of Guanajuato, the
town captured in 1810 by the village
priest Miguel Hidalgo, father of Mexico's
independence.

162, 163. The smiling faces of children are to be seen everywhere in Mexico, whether beside an echinocactus in the desert of Sonora or with mother and grandmother in the Yucatán. The three generations of women in the Yucatán wear huipiles, the loose, flowing garment that has come down from the Maya.

164. *A tattered net, a ball, active children – enough to make a game. Some 80 per cent of the population are under forty years of age. At the present growth rate, one million new jobs need to be created each year to provide work for those coming onto the labour market.*

165, 166. Mexico City's bullring is claimed to be the largest ever built. At four in the afternoon each Sunday from October to March, up to 60,000 spectators gather there. Bullfighters come from Spain and the rest of Latin America to perform in Mexico's Plaza de Toros.

167, 168. Bullfighting was introduced to Mexico by the Spaniards. At its best, it is as spectacular here as anywhere in the world. At its worst, it is little more than costumed butchery. Today, soccer may have the bigger audience, but there are many who still have their permanent seats in the ring.

169. The Metro in the Mexican capital has some trains underground, some on the surface. It is clean, cheap and efficient. Eight lines crisscross the city. Each station has a name and also an easily recognized symbol – important in view of the level of illiteracy in the capital.

170. Perhaps one of those who never learned to read and write. An Indian, with a timeless face, from Chiapas, the land of the last of the Maya.

171. Another survivor from the past: a mining train in Baja California. Once used to carry copper ore, it now rusts slowly. Baja California is a wealthy state, but now most of its income comes from 'in-bond' manufacturing agreements with the United States and from tourism.

172. With her lined face and work-worn hands, this Mexican woman sits pensively before a cathedral door. In her lifetime, the country has passed through a full-scale revolution, many presidents, millions of births and deaths.

174. Two men of the people are popular heroes of the revolution: Pancho Villa, the bandit from the north, and Emiliano Zapata, the melon grower from the south, led peasant armies against the State.

173. Old men with their rifles and their memories of times past sit in the sun before the Farmacía Esperanza, the Pharmacy of Hope.

175. Many Mexicans see themselves as cowboys, riders of the purple sage. They dress in expensive outfits that glitter with gold and silver, and wear sombreros the size of tables. Known as charros, on holidays and display days they give exhibitions of superb horsemanship all over the country.

176, 177. This statue of José Maria Morelos, one of the fathers of the country's independence, presents him as a vaquero, a Hollywood cowboy, rather than the sturdy guerrilla leader he really was. Morelos' plan for social reform after independence was one of the most enlightened the world has ever seen. It has never been fully carried out.

178. Along the border with the United States stretches a customs-free 'in-bond' manufacturing zone, where Mexicans assemble goods for American producers in plants known as maquiladoras. This benefits both sides: Mexicans have jobs and Americans, lower labour costs than at home.

179, 180. Most of the workers in the maquiladoras are women. They turn out auto parts, shoes, electrical goods, inexpensive jewelry anything that needs nimble fingers. Their wages are more than welcome in a country where unemployment runs well into double figures. As a result, thousands have drifted north, swelling the population of the border towns.

*181, 182. Guitars and trumpets are the
principal instruments of the mariachis,
the travelling musicians who play on the
spot or go with you where you will.
Violins and harps also appear, especially
if the music has the flavour of Veracruz,
a gentler, lapping melody, like the waves
themselves on this southern shore.*

183. A couple off to the fiesta, he in his smart new hat, she in a huipil, the simple dress that was worn before the Spaniards came. Some huipiles are densely embroidered, others are picked out with flowers and leaves. All are feminine, comfortable and softly flattering.

184, 185. At intersections in Mexico City, where traffic lights hold an audience captive, street vendors and performers display their wares, their talents, their sidewalk skills. You can buy a Virgin, watch clowns perform, or see a man breathe fire.

186. Eyes of the future, eyes of hope. A child gazes through a decorated window, past the painted flowers, into what lies mistily ahead in Mexico's overcrowded capital.

187. In every Mexican's heart there is a
fiesta waiting to be celebrated. At times,
especially if the occasion is religious, they
dress with great solemnity, wearing styles,
often actual garments, that have been
passed down through generations. Each
town and village has its patron saint,
whose feast is celebrated to the full.

188, 189. *Trumpets and drums, food and fireworks, horsemen splendidly dressed on magnificent animals – all elements that bring joy to the festive heart. In the centres of cities and in remote villages alike, fiestas sometimes last for days.*

190. *Clearing lake weed from Pátzcuaro, where the once-clean waters, teeming with delicate whitefish, have become sadly overgrown and polluted. The lakeside town of Pátzcuaro, halfway between Guadalajara and Mexico City, is still one of the most picturesque in the world.*

191. *A typical village house on Lake Pátzcuaro in Michoacán, a beautiful but still poor and underdeveloped state.*

192. *Mexican pottery is among the most original and colourful in all Latin America. At times crude, at times exquisite, it is always interesting – as full of character as the people who fashion it.*

193, 194. *Mexicans are a gregarious people, seldom solitary. They gather whenever possible even in disconsolate pairs contemplating their problems. They congregate in swirling crowds to witness any event. But most of all they come together at fiestas with music and dancing, their faces wreathed in smiles.*

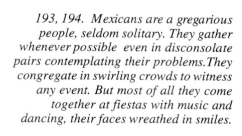

195. In Mexico City, crowds watch dance teams perform on a national holiday. They are moving to the rhythms of rancheras, the country and western music of northern Mexico. 'Native' dancing ranges from the Spanish formal to the wilder coastal flings. Often it is organized, like the above, rather than purely spontaneous.

196. *Xochimilco, south-east of Mexico City, where waterways that were originally part of Tenochtitlán, city of the Aztecs, cut through fruit and flower gardens. On holidays, flower-decorated punts can be hired for a floating picnic.*

197. *The boats, above, on Lake Chapala near Guadalajara are for picnics, fishing or wildfowl shooting. It was near Chapala, in the town of Sayula, that D.H. Lawrence wrote his Mexican novel 'The Plumed Serpent'.*

198. *Other sites for other sports. A golf course at Guaymas in the state of Sonora.*

War with the United States

It was a war that should never have happened. This might be said about many wars, but it is especially applicable here. It was not a just war. Many prominent Americans were against it. Abraham Lincoln, then a young congressman, opposed it bitterly, mainly because the excuse for the war was Texas – and Texas was a state that permitted the ownership of slaves.

Mexico, incidentally, had abolished black slavery in 1828, eighteen years before the war with the United States began.

The problem of Texas had never been solved. The document signed by Santa Anna after his capture at Lynchburg Ferry carried little weight with the Mexican government, which did not accept the independence of the Lone Star Republic, recognized by the United States, Great Britain and France. For some years there was a sort of stalemate. Then, in 1845, a new American president came to power.

In his inaugural address, James K. Polk declared that the United States had 'clear and unquestionable' title to Oregon and Texas. The latter was admitted to the Union, and Mexico broke off diplomatic relations.

Just over a year after his election, Polk persuaded the American Congress to declare war.

For a while there were American advances and Mexican stands of resistance. Both sides claimed victories. The Americans were better equipped, but less able to withstand the rigours of the climate and local diseases. The Mexicans, particularly their conscript armies, fought bravely. Neither side had great leadership in the field. The American commander was General Zachary Taylor, known as 'Old Rough and Ready', later to become the twelfth president of the United States. Recently his body was exhumed in an attempt to discover whether or not he had been poisoned. It seems that he might have been, although it is doubtful if this has any connection with his time in Mexico.

There were several Mexican generals in the early stages of the war, leadership was confused until the government decided it was time to recall – you are right – General Antonio López de Santa Anna, at the time suffering a further term of disgrace and exile to Cuba.

However, his country needed him now, and, once again, Santa Anna displayed his Machiavellian talent to take control of the scene. He was in Cuba when called, on the wrong side of the American blockade. In order to return to Mexico, Santa Anna wrote to President Polk offering to mediate if the Americans would let him through. Amazingly, Polk accepted.

As soon as his foot – he only had one now – touched Mexican soil, Santa Anna began organizing the army. Some six months later he was ready. He rode north and attacked General Taylor's forces. In what the Mexicans call the Battle of Angostura he almost ended the war... Many fought bravely, many died, neither side gained a decisive victory, though both commanders were honoured as heroes.

Perhaps Santa Anna could have claimed the day, but in another of those curious Mexican hesitations, as with Hidalgo when Mexico City lay before him, he failed to follow through. He led his men away in the night.

After that the war began in earnest. Under the command of General Winfield Scot, on March 7, 1847, ten thousand American soldiers landed at Veracruz. Like Hernán Cortés before them, they marched into the Valley of Mexico, taking the same route as the Spaniard did, between the twin volcanoes, Ixtacíhuatl and Popocatépetl.

An intriguing confrontation occurred in Puebla, a splendid old city, some one hundred miles south-east of the capital, where today they make beautiful pottery. There, in 1847, General Scot contacted Santa Anna and

199. A mariachi guitar player fortifying himself with a little tequila. 'Mariachi' is from the French word 'marriage'; these musicians played at weddings. Tequila is from the fermented heart of the agave cactus. Heady mariachi music and tequila can be a dangerous combination.

asked about the mediation the Mexican was supposed to be arranging. Santa Anna replied that he needed time and a little more money to 'persuade' certain diehards to change their minds. Once again the Americans had the wool pulled over their eyes. Ten thousand dollars was handed over, money which Santa Anna used to bolster Mexican defences.

To little avail, however. The American advance continued. By September, through the downpours of the rainy season, they made their way to the centre of Mexico City. Their last battle was against children. On the hill in Chapultepec Park, where today so many Mexican families picnic, cadets from the military college made a final stand against the American invaders.

The Niños Heroes, the Boy Heroes, as they came to be known, fought against some of the men who were to become leading players in the American Civil War. Robert E. Lee was one of them, so was Ulysses S. Grant. The cadets were defeated, of course, and a number, refusing to surrender, jumped from the heights of Chapultepec to their deaths on the rocks below.

After that it was over. Santa Anna fought a few more skirmishes, then fell out with the President and returned to exile, to the shadows from which he had emerged. By the peace treaty signed in 1848, Mexico lost California, Nevada, Arizona, Colorado, most of New Mexico and Utah – half of the territory it had called its own. The United States government paid a token fifteen million dollars for the land, a fraction of its real worth.

And Santa Anna waited. One day he would be back.

Juárez and Maximilian

After peace with the United States had been signed in 1848, after the money had been paid and the northern territories lost, politics by Mexican standards entered a period of relative calm, even reform. Of course presidents came and went, some faster than others, but an eye was being cast toward a more stable future, and thought was being given to a more even distribution of wealth and power.

In Mexico, as in many other parts of the world, the two principal wielders of power had been the Army and the Church. Down through the coils of time, the men with the arms and those who mediated with the gods had held the reins of authority, not to mention immense wealth and property.

Of the two, the Church was by far the more stable. Armies might break and shatter, generals rise or fade, but the Church was a constant factor, and the wealth it had accrued was great. Mexico had always been a Catholic country. During Spanish colonial rule, its priests were part of the process. In the independent land, Catholicism was the state religion.

The Spanish Inquisition had established an office in Mexico City in 1571, but its punishments were relatively mild by European standards. There was little danger of converted Indians returning to their ancient gods, for most of the old images had been destroyed. Desperate for some belief to cling to, they had accepted Christianity.

In fact, Christianity in Mexico then, as today, often displayed a marrying of old and new, a remarkably theatrical mixture of pagan imagery and Christian thought. You are unlikely to see anywhere a bloodier Christ than those hanging on the walls of some Mexican churches. Red rivers gush from the wounds in torrents. The flagellants in the silver town of Tasco beat their backs to shreds. On the Day of the Dead, November 2, All Souls' Day, food is laid out on the graves of loved ones, offerings are made to departed souls. The night before, graveyards all over the country glow with candlelight, the dead are spoken to, and children feast on skulls and skeletons made of sugar.

This blending is understandable, for it bridged the gap between what was being offered and what had been taken away. The missionaries who came after the conquistadores based the hymns they taught on Indian chants.

However, as the power, and particularly the wealth, of the Church grew, it was increasingly resented. Santa Anna had forced loans from the Church, loans he had no intention of repaying. He returned, by the way, for a year on the presidential throne in 1853, when he had himself referred to as His Most Supreme Highness, spent what he could find in the Treasury, and sold the Mesilla Valley, now part of Arizona, for ten million dollars. Then he slipped away into exile once again, this time to Venezuela, saying he was handing back power to the people.

He was to be allowed back again in 1872, an old man now, his tempestuous days behind him. He died, some say penniless, but this is hard to believe – he was far too astute for that. When he died he was eighty-one, remarkable, years old.

The man who rose out of the ranks to follow Santa Anna down the path of history was of a very different character. Benito Juárez, sometimes referred to as the Lincoln of Mexico, a full-blooded Zapotec Indian, was to give Mexico its first taste of real democracy, and was to issue the order that put Maximilian, the French puppet, last Emperor of Mexico, before a firing squad.

Juárez, born in Oaxaca, spoke no Spanish until he was twelve, when he went to Oaxaca City as a servant. From that moment there was no turning back. He studied law, entered public service and, in 1847, became governor of the state. He seems to have always been a liberal thinker and, perhaps because of his humble background, to have felt the material wealth of the Church, its property, its trappings, its exemption from tax, to be unjust. It was a belief that drove him all his life.

After spending some time in exile in New Orleans in the company of other liberal minds, he returned to Mexico and was made Minister of Justice under the presidency of Ignacio Comonfort. In 1857 he drafted a law intended to curb the privileges of both the Church and the Army. Its main focus was to compel the Church to sell its estates to private buyers.

It went down like a lead balloon.

J. Clemente Orozco: ‹Images of the Revolution›

The Church protested vigorously, using all the powers at its command. Any public official who swore obedience to the law was threatened with excommunication. Anyone who bought church property was denied the right to confess his sins or to receive the Holy Sacrament. In a Catholic country, where even the most liberal thinkers had been brought up in the Faith, the law acted as a catalyst for further bloodshed and disaster. Fighting broke out. The War of Reform had begun.

Juárez was imprisoned by conservative troops rebelling against the new law, but escaped and established himself in Veracruz. The conservatives held Mexico City. Throughout three long and bitter years of war Juárez remained intractable. In spite of the chaos, the cruelty with which the war was fought, Juárez was unswerving in his beliefs.

During the fighting he was supported by the United States, while most of the European powers recognized his conservative opponents. This taking of sides had long-term implications and, in the end, was to spark another war.

By January 7, 1861, the War of Reform had come to an end, and Mexico was once again shattered and bankrupt. In all its turbulent history it had rarely sunk as low. A War of Reform it may have been in name, but there was nothing enlightened about the way it had been conducted. Both sides had shot prisoners as a matter of course. Banditry was commonplace. The damage done to books, whole libraries, gold and silver churchware, was on a scale that can only be compared with the ruthlessness of the Spanish conquistadores when they first plundered the land. The Church had lost property, priceless possessions; the State had lost something of its soul. Both were bankrupt. Both were bereft.

And, over all, president now, hung the impassive face of Benito Pablo Juárez, a short, dark man who wore dark clothes, and in none of his portraits does he smile. Nothing was to alter his conviction that church property must be shared. His ideas, the laws he formulated, extend to the present day. All ecclesiastical buildings, except churches in which Mass was said, were confiscated. Monasteries were abolished. Civil marriage became official, rather than that of the Church. It was only in 1991 that these laws saw any relaxation. Under President Carlos Salinas de Gortari, Mexican Congress voted to end these anticlerical policies. The Church is again permitted to own property, priests and nuns can wear their habits in the street. Until the recent change of heart, men and women of the Church were obliged to dress like the laity when they set foot outside their door.

But if Benito Juárez had won the battle on the homefront, his troubles with the outside world had only just begun.

Three European nations, though they knew Mexico was frail, or because they recognized its weakness, pressed heavily for the repayment of debts. This was not the first time such demands had been made, nor was it to be the last. Today Mexico's debt is enormous. But then, in 1862, the country, in its delicate state of recovery, was invaded by foreign forces.

Spanish troops, soon joined by forces from France and Great Britain, landed at Veracruz and took control of the city. Another war was about to begin.

Financial claims against Mexico have never been conducted in a civilized manner. In the early days of the Republic after Iturbide, the first emperor, had been deposed, Great Britain had poured money into Mexico to re-finance the old Spanish silver mines, hoping to lay hands on the vast wealth the earth contained. Cornishmen populated the countryside. Cornish pasties are still served today. But savagery over debt repayment poisoned Mexico's relationship with overseas lenders for many years.

Sketch, detail of the Cathedral
of Guadalajara.

The French had been harsher in their debt collecting. The Pastry War, where Santa Anna lost a leg and regained popularity, had been launched to settle claims for cash. But the landing that took place in 1862 was a vastly more serious affair. Before it was over Mexico had been virtually reconquered and Maximilian, the last emperor, installed.

For some time France had had its eyes on Mexico. This rich and, as the French saw it, savage country seemed to be a prize quite easily gained. Napoleon III, then Emperor of France, had been approached by a group of Mexican royalists who encouraged him to believe that the installation of an emperor, someone of European breeding and background, was what unruly Mexico needed to solve its problems. It was just a matter of finding the right man for the job.

So when the force landed at Veracruz the French, at least, were in search of much more than a down-payment and promises for the rest – they wanted Mexico. They had their man for the imperial throne: the Hapsburg Archduke Ferdinand Maximilian, an honest, doomed and illusioned man who was to die facing a firing squad against a church wall in Querétaro, some one hundred and sixty miles north of Mexico City.

After France, Spain and Great Britain landed their contingents in Veracruz in 1862, France's true intentions became clear, and Spain and Great Britain withdrew. French forces pressed ahead, but, surprised at the ferocity of the resistance they encountered, when they reached the city of Puebla, south of Mexico City, were driven all the way back to the coast. In celebration of the victory, *el Cinco de Mayo,* the Fifth of May, is still a national holiday.

However, the French returned, and with an army of some thirty thousand men, many of them zouaves, fierce Algerian fighters who, in their bright red pantaloons, became the terror of the Mexican countryside. Juárez and his cabinet fled north to San Luis Potosí. For the next three years his men fought battle after battle against the determined invaders. Juárez fought wherever he was able, from retreats and hide-aways all over the north of Mexico.

In 1864 Maximilian and his consort, Empress Carlota, arrived in Mexico City. Their splendid palace, a royal European mansion built on Mexican soil, became the centre of their lives. Although Maximilian spoke Spanish, dressed like a Mexican and ate Mexican food, he was desperately out of place. He failed to understand why the Mexican people did not receive him with open arms, as he had been led to believe. He retreated to his palace, gave lavish balls, banquets and luncheons, while Mexicans died fighting his troops.

By the end of 1865, Napoleon III, having realized that his incursion into Mexico was a disastrous mistake, ordered the withdrawal of his troops and the war swung the other way. Carlota journeyed to France in an unsuccessful attempt to persuade Napoleon to change his mind. She went to Rome, but the Pope did nothing to help her. She became convinced, not without reason, that there were plots against her and was declared insane. (She died, at the age of eighty-seven, in 1927.)

When he knew the French army was leaving, Maximilian refused the chance to join them. Somewhere among his crumbling dreams was an image of himself as the man that Mexico needed. He surrendered to Juárez and was executed: the most damning evidence against him was his signature on an order authorizing the shooting of Mexican prisoners of war.

Juárez was once more president, his rule was law. But another star was rising on the Mexican horizon – that of José de la Cruz Porfirio Díaz, whose influence was to be felt over the land for the next thirty-four years.

Revolution

The Turn of Porfirio Díaz

Benito Juárez was an iron-faced, dark-skinned Indian; Porfirio Díaz was lighter-skinned and wore a large moustache. The first was an angel in Mexican memory; the second became its most controversial figure.

Neither was absolutely the colour Mexican history has painted him. Both shaped much of what Mexico is today.

Benito Juárez died suddenly in office in 1872, probably of a heart attack, according to some with the pen of democracy clutched in his fingers.

Porfirio Díaz came to power in 1876. Apart for one brief period he ruled Mexico until 1911, the year after the start of the Revolution that saw Pancho Villa and Emiliano Zapata ride through the columns of history. Porfirio Díaz began as a follower of Juárez, he ended as a friend of big business. As far as he was concerned, Mexico needed outside money, expertise and efficiency. He encouraged it quite openly, and Mexico was once again invaded – this time by capitalists, most of them American or English.

Porfirio Díaz came from part-Indian stock and, like Juárez, was born in Oaxaca. His early career was distinguished by heroism. He fought the French, was captured and, like the hero of an adventure tale, escaped with the aid of a lasso. He was in command of the forces that re-took the city of Mexico a few days after Emperor Maximilian was shot. He was there when Juárez returned and was sadly disillusioned when the latter barely thanked him for what he had done.

Perhaps this, in part, turned Díaz away from the liberal camp. He retired to Oaxaca and waited. After Juárez died, he challenged the successor, Lerdo, when he offered himself for a second term. Pledging effective suffrage and no re-election, Díaz took the city by storm. It was not a pledge he was to uphold: he himself was voted into office eight times.

His dictum, however, remains in force today. Mexican presidents serve one six-year term. Some criticize this on the grounds that the man in charge has but one chance to make his name and fortune, and this often leads to abuse of authority.

Once in power, in 1876, Díaz certainly made his name. In his time he was called the greatest figure in the whole American continent, and that included Theodore Roosevelt. He achieved peace throughout the country, very harshly at times. He brought wealth to Mexico, at some cost: society was split in two. But the foundations of Mexican industry were laid by Don Porfirio, as he come to be known. Don, in Spanish, is a common title of respect, somewhat like the English Esquire, which seems to have vanished in this day and age.

Díaz underwent his own personal changes. The rough army leader, the part-Indian who escaped from a cell by sliding down a rope, become one of the gentry. The semi-educated fighter, who once had to sneak back into Mexico disguised as a workman, turned into a model of conservatism. He married a cultured creole girl much younger than himself, who helped to reshape her husband while he reshaped the nation.

From his election as president in 1876 until he reached the end of his long career, Díaz never once looked back. Nor did Mexico – economically. Between 1880 and 1910 it turned from a country ripped apart by war and plunder into a modern manufacturing nation. With the considerable help of foreign advisors, an efficient banking system was developed. Industries mushroomed. Railways linked north and south, east and west. In 1876 there were only four hundred miles of railway track in the whole of Mexico. There were nearly twelve thousand by the end of Díaz's term.

The mining industry was reborn. Mineral exports rose by six hundred and fifty per cent during the Díaz era. The list of developmental works seems endless: electric power and light, telephones and telegraphs, drainage and waterworks, agriculture and real estate, and every sort of industry, heavy or light. Every money-making enterprise appeared to flourish while Porfirio Díaz ruled the country.

And rule it he did. He was not a tall man, but he towered over the landscape. His police force operated with what was, quite often, deadly efficiency. In the countryside, in areas riddled with banditry, his men organized a force that come to be feared. They were ruthless, but they made travel a little safer, especially for the foreigners who were bringing so much wealth and expertise into the country.

Díaz was a dictator in many ways, some benign, some that knew no mercy. As far as the Church was concerned, especially with regard to the recent Juárez laws prohibiting ownership of property and abolishing monasteries, Díaz left the legal documents as they were, but made no effort to put these decrees into practice. Catholic schools were revived. The voices of the bishops were heard in the land.

And with all the technical skill that he had at his fingertips, Porfirio Díaz retackled the age-old problem of Mexico City – its lack of foundation, its tendency to sink gently into the Aztec mud, down among the bones of the Spanish conquistadores who lay there, their pockets still laden with plundered gold. A new canal was built and worked for a while, but the Aztec gods are hard to please – it failed to solve the problem. In 1969 more work was done, yet still the beautiful Bellas Artes fades inch by sinking inch.

The same English company then constructed a rather more permanent monument to the Díaz administration. Across the narrow neck of land between the Gulf of Mexico and the Pacific, before the land swells again to include Yucatán and Guatemala, two hundred miles of brand new railway were built, with an equally new port at either end – Mexico's equivalent to the Panama Canal. At the north end is Coatzacoalcos, in the south, Salina Cruz. Laying the line must have been ghastly work. I once spent a hot and steamy night in a cheap hotel in Salina Cruz – even the mosquitoes were sweating.

A typical nineteenth-century Mexican wine-shop.

It was under the Díaz administration that Mexico's oil fields were developed. At the beginning of the twentieth century Americans began buying oil-bearing land, extensions of the Texan fields, in the states of Tamaulipas and San Luis Potosí. When the railway was being cut across to Salina Cruz, oil was seen seeping from the earth. More concessions were purchased. Then even richer strikes were made in Veracruz and Tabasco. Mexico's black gold, and sometimes its curse, began to pour from the wells that were bored.

Oil has proved to be the country's biggest earner, now bringing in something like four billion dollars a year. It has also been a hurdle over which the Mexican economy has tripped and stumbled. In the boom years, the late 1970s, international banks fell over themselves to offer the Mexican government loans. They saw oil prices rising, and thought the boom would go on forever. When prices faltered and fell and the banks wanted their money back, or the high interest rates guaranteed, Mexico was unable to comply. Not all the money that had been borrowed had been wisely spent. Mexico's economic star faded to a dimness from which it is only just emerging.

In 1975 the peso traded at 12.5 to the U.S. dollar, as it had for something like twenty years, but by the early 1990s, the rate was 3,000 to the dollar. Mexico is recovering today, but the struggle has been long and slow and hard.

However, Porfirio Díaz in his day envisaged nothing but progress. He wanted a stable country in which money could be made and he had the power, a land of limitless opportunity.

In his eagerness to encourage foreign capital, Díaz issued concessions that were often shortsighted, even crippling, and sowed the seeds of revolution. Money was made by the ton in Mexico – most of it went overseas. Dividends were paid to foreign investors, interest was demanded on loans. Industrialists and investors in New York, London and Paris got richer, the poor in Mexico were left even poorer than they had been before the boom. In spite of the fortune flowing overseas, Mexico's Treasury benefited also, for the first time since independence achieving a balanced budget. Yet the workers, especially those on the great estates, in the mines and lumber camps, earned less than ever in terms of buying power.

Porfirio Díaz might have had a balanced budget, but he had an unbalanced country. And any protests against the way things were run were mercilessly suppressed. In the early 1900s a strike in the northern copper town of Cananea, in the state of Sonora, was put down by government troops with considerable loss of life. When textile workers rose up to decry their conditions, the miserable wages they were being paid, in factories near Orizaba, inland from Veracruz, more troops were called in – two hundred workers died.

These may have been some of the worst cases, but even under better conditions life for the worker, the *peon* on the land, was grim, all too often hopeless. Corporal punishment was normal; hacienda owners took their whips to their workers as they did to their beasts of burden. Diet was pitiful, housing primitive, and no change seemed in sight. Education, especially for farm-workers' children, was practically non-existent.

And while all this was going on, the Indians were losing their land. Down through the windings of history, regardless of who was in power, most Mexican Indians had relied on their right to the land. Before the conquest there was a system known broadly as *calpulli* which allotted a set amount of land to each family or tribe. The Spanish Laws of the Indies respected this. Mexican independence intended to see this basic right reinforced.

But Porfirio Díaz denied the Indians the part of Mexico that was theirs. By the time Díaz came to power, these communal Indian lands – or what they had left to them – were known as *ejidos*. In the mid-nineteenth century, hacienda development had grabbed much *ejido* land, and by the beginning of the twentieth century the Indians had largely been dispossessed. During the Díaz years no less than one hundred and twenty-five million acres were sold to private owners, much of it Indian land, much of it to people who never set foot on it or had much idea what it was like.

When the Indian owners, some of whom had titles going back hundreds of years, protested, the *rurales* rode in and moved them on. Revolts were stamped out before they began. The new owners, especially those who had never even taken a lungful of Mexican air, were known as *latifundistas* – the absent landlords to whom the money went.

And this, basically, explains the success of the Mexican Revolution, that bloody, unruly, relentless revolt between 1910 and 1920, with all its heroes, its heroines, its men on white horses, its villains. The uprising triumphed, toppled the economically-balanced Mexico of Díaz, because the people wanted their land back, because Mexicans wanted Mexico. They wanted their property taken out of the hands of the great hacienda owners and the absentee landlords – they wanted to give Mexico back to their children.

A Decade of Bloodshed

The fall of Porfirio Díaz was, in part, of his own making, a sort of political own-goal. He was old, close to eighty, and beginning to make mistakes. He offended the United States in little ways, but he astounded his own country by telling an American journalist that he would not stand for an eighth term. Perhaps he thought his words would never reach Mexican ears, perhaps he imagined that it was merely part of a conversation. Whatever, when he did run for the eighth time and, of course, won, his major opponent, Francisco Indalécio Madero became instrumental in the downfall of the man who had ruled Mexico for thirty-four hard years.

Madero was no hero on a white horse. He was an unimpressive little man, just over five feet, who was a teetotaller, a spiritualist and a vegetarian. A lot of people did not take him seriously. Díaz put him in jail and then let him go.

But Madero had written a book. He was the well-educated son of a northern hacienda owner, had been to school and college in Baltimore and Paris, and his book *The Presidential Succession of 1910*, although considered somewhat mediocre, was to alter the course of Mexican history.

Although not a highly literate country, then or now, Mexico responded to the publication. Its main message, much of which must have passed by word of mouth, was that there should be 'Effective Suffrage and No Re-election'. This was what Porfirio Díaz had promised in 1876, and then ignored completely. It became a new rallying cry in 1910, and today is dear to every Mexican's political heart. All government letters, between the text and the signature of the sender, carry the message. It was a challenge that Díaz took personally – it landed Madero in prison, although it did not stop him running for president.

After failing against Díaz in the 1910 election, in which he was 'accorded' a total of one hundred and ninety-six votes, Madero fled to San Antonio, Texas, and set up a revolutionary council. The council issued what was called the Plan of San Luis Potosí, named Madero as provisional president, and called for an uprising on November 20.

There was no uprising. A few minor disturbances took place, but these were becoming commonplace. However, there is no doubt that a revolution had begun. Its course was to be decided by three men – a bandit and a shopkeeper in the north, a peasant in the south, not one of whom had much in common with the book-writer, Madero.

In the north the *pistolero* Pancho Villa and the shopkeeper Pascual Orozco stormed Ciudad Juárez, the city known as El Paso in the U.S.A. They took it on May 10, 1911, after Madero had talked to Díaz's ministers and got nothing in return. Madero had, in fact, issued an order against the storming of the city, but by now he was out of his depth.

Two days later, in the south, Emiliano Zapata with an army of fellow-peasants took the mountain town of Cuautla in the state of Morelos. From that moment there was no turning back. Mexico was never to be the same again.

While these three men had been organizing forces, Díaz celebrated like the lord he was in Mexico City. There were two reasons for the enormous fiestas. He had himself to glorify – eighty years old, eight times president, still, on the surface, master of all. He had his country to honour – it had been one hundred years since Hidalgo had uttered his cry for independence.

Edition of the ‹Mexican Modern Review›, with poet
Salvador Díaz Mirón on the cover page.

Distinguished guests came from all over the world to drink their toasts to Mexico. They danced at balls at the National Palace, on one occasion drinking twenty rail-waggons of champagne. They watched Porfirio Díaz drive in state down the Paseo de la Reforma, the central artery of Mexico City, they saw the Independence Column, in the same avenue, unveiled to reveal its golden Winged Victory – the Angel, the Mexicans call the statue. When it fell in the earthquake of 1957 and did not break, many said that God still smiled on the city.

But not in the second decade of this same century. Within six months the country was trembling, and Díaz was to relinquish power. After Orozco, Villa and Zapata had made their demands known, Treasury Minister Limantour signed an agreement for the President's departure. At first the old man objected violently and ordered troops to fire on the crowds demonstrating outside the National Palace. Two hundred died, but Díaz went. He fled to Paris where he died four years later, a sick old man whose name has been reviled in Mexican history ever since.

After Díaz left, blood really began to flow. As happens so often after years of repression, a sort of madness tore Mexico apart. Violence sprang up on every side, brutality and betrayal seemed to be the order of the day.

Perhaps the murderous chaos of the Mexican Revolution was so intense because there was no clear philosophy behind the movement. No Marx or Lenin. No Robespierre. Plans were issued, declarations were made, but there was no unity of ideas among those who controlled the bloody machine that was beginning to roll forward. The men at the top were poles apart in character, background and ambitions. At times they thought only of themselves.

Madero, the rich intellectual, had little knowledge of the terrible racial and social complications of the forces he had unleashed. Like wild dogs they ran while he, when elected president in 1911, felt he had achieved what he had set out to do – to unseat the dictator Díaz. In his government he re-employed ministers that had served in the Díaz cabinet. He gave command of the army to General Victoriano Huerta, another Díaz faithful, a man who could not have proved more treacherous. In the end, Huerta had Madero murdered and took the presidency himself.

Orozco, the shopkeeper, saw his fortunes rise and fall. After taking Ciudad Juárez with Pancho Villa, he fell out with Madero, believing he had not been adequately rewarded. In 1912 he set his men against government forces and was routed by General Huerta. He later joined Huerta and when the latter fell, Orozco escaped to the United States, where he was shot down as a common outlaw.

Pancho Villa remained a bandit all his life. In is doubtful if any political ideal ever entered his head. He fought for Madero because it suited him. He fought with Orozco and then against him. He fought with Huerta, was courtmartialled for insubordination and condemned to die, but was given another chance – this time to fight against Huerta. He was more flamboyant than most, but sadly typical of the outlaw opportunists who controlled the hard, dry north. He is remembered for his brutality, his temper, the way he changed his mind, and for devising an economical method of shooting prisoners. He lined them up, three deep, and used one bullet to despatch all three! He died as violently as he had lived – in a hail of machine-gun bullets, in 1923, killed by those who wanted to repay him in kind for what he had done. Today he is one of the colourful revolutionaries; Mexico has forgiven him his crimes. But it was not until 1967, nearly fifty years after the Revolution was over, that his name was added to the roster of heroes in Mexico's Chamber of Deputies.

Of the three who rode with their rifles in the first days of the uprising, only Emiliano Zapata seemed to have any sense of the future. His Plan of Ayala, written by a schoolmaster in Cuautla, in 1911, demanded the return of Indian lands to the people, but whether that demand was based on justice or a hatred of the owners of the great haciendas is open to question. He was another man who never smiled when his photograph was being taken.

Pancho Villa, on the other hand, seemed to be laughing all the time. On the only occasion the two men met, they were photographed together – Villa, broadly smiling, seated in the presidential chair, Zapata beside him, curled into himself, suspicion in every line of his body. They came together uneasily, linked by a common hatred of Venustiano Carranza, a tall, bearded figure from the north who looked like an Old Testament prophet. Carranza, self-styled First Chief of the Constitutionalist Army, fought against both Villa and Zapata.

The years between 1912 and 1916 were confused and violent throughout the land. Like feudal lords, the various leaders remained much within their territories. Villa plundered the north. Zapata fought in the south. New faces, names, political plans appeared and were over-ridden, lost or forgotten. Nowhere was there any order. At times the bands fought together, mostly they operated alone. Villa and Zapata planned a combined attack on Carranza when the First Chief was in Veracruz. It might have succeeded, had Zapata not stopped and turned away. In another of those Mexican decisions, he decided to go no further than the city of Puebla; he felt lost beyond the mountains of his home state of Morelos. Pancho Villa stopped too, and Carranza got away. Villa went back to Mexico City and spent a month there, a month of activities that did not improve his image or popularity.

And while the rifles fired and the horses galloped and the rebel-soldiers yelled, there was little of any substance for the people, nothing for Mexico. Round after round of infighting and betrayal, with barely a noble thought involved, offered little to the common man – the Indian, the peasant, the *peon* – apart from sudden death. In the second decade of this century the population of Mexico dropped by several hundreds of thousands.

Few of the leaders died peacefully in their beds: Madero was murdered by Huerta; Villa was machine-gunned down; Orozco was shot as a common outlaw; Zapata, lured into an ambush, died by rifle-fire, at the hands of Carranza's men. Carranza, himself, after being elected president and realizing that his regime was about to fall, fled Mexico City with a train full of booty. If he had not been so greedy, he might have got away. Like the conquistadores before him, his love of gold was his undoing. Caught on his sluggish journey, he was shot at night. Of those who fought, betrayed, and fought again, it seems that Huerta alone had the distinction of dying in bed, albeit a prisoner in El Paso. He died from hepatitis, in 1916, facing south, looking down toward a Mexico that was no longer his.

The list of presidents grew longer. Some, for a time, were enlightened. Carranza produced a new constitution, a sweeping document which should have put Mexico's problems to rest. It was the most progressive legislation in the world, providing for an eight-hour day, a minimum wage, profit-sharing, and the right to strike. All *ejido* lands taken away from the people were to be restored. The anti-Church legislation of Juárez was brought back. It became illegal for clerics to own property; even their ecclesiastical clothes belonged, in name, to the State. Carranza's constitution was as big and as bold as the mural by González Camarena which celebrates it on the wall of the National History Museum, in Chapultepec Castle. Unfortunately it did not last as long.

The white-bearded prophet made some effort to put the constitution into practice, but not enough. Like Madero before him, once in office he lost his drive. He became intolerant, obstinate and reluctant to give up power. He refused to name as his successor Alvaro Obregón, who had been his right-hand man, standing beside him year after year. Another rebellion followed. Carranza fled and was shot in the middle of the night.

Obregón the Practical President

Alvaro Obregón, who became President of Mexico in 1920, had been a schoolteacher and a clever general. Unlike many of his fellow-revolutionaries, he knew how to read and write. Of Irish ancestry, he was descended from Michael O'Brien, a bodyguard to the last of the Spanish viceroys. He was the youngest of eighteen children and came from the state of Sonora, northern hacienda country, a vast territory between Chihuahua and Baja California. The revolution had touched some of the great properties there, but had barely affected their wealth. One of the cattle-barons, who rode in a gold-trimmed coach pulled by white horses, when asked by a Chicago meat company if he could supply them immediately with fifteen hundred cattle, replied with a certain irony: 'What colour?'.

Obregón was forty when he finally sat in the presidential chair. He had grown up in the hacienda-rich north, a part of the country that had boomed under Porfirio Díaz. He had seen much of Mexico destroyed in the years of revolution, bandits and feudal chieftains burning property, blowing up rail track, taking lives. He had witnessed his country turning into tribal fiefdoms. He had also fought against Pancho Villa and lost an arm in battle.

Now with the power to make changes, he put into process his belief that what Mexico needed was a sense of security, the knowledge that its citizens could work and settle with some hope of a future. And as a realist he knew how this could be brought about – every man has his price.

Out of this pragmatism, this matter-of-fact approach, has grown the Mexico of today with all its colour and brightness, with all its shadows in the corridors of power. In Obregón's day little attempt was made to disguise the greasing of the wheels, the deals that were done with money or property, with governmental offices, with presidential favours. And for a while it worked. A new breed of money-makers came into being, men who gained large slices of industry and commerce, plantations and mines. Jobs were provided with some security of tenure and, most cleverly of all, the goals, the dreams, the promises of so many revolutionary manifestoes, were put sluggishly into practice. Token allotments of *ejido*-lands were returned to the people. Trade unions were allowed to form.

The crippled economy began to inch forward, to crawl into gear again. When he had time to look around, Obregón discovered that Mexico's industries, its oil, mining, railways, banks and public utilities, were still the property of foreign investors, as they had been in the days of Díaz, the only difference being that then Mexico had enjoyed good international links with the countries of her owners. By the time Obregón came along, these had been soured by years of bloodshed. Nevertheless he began to repay the bondholders, returns on capital were resumed. After years of suspicion of revolutionary regimes, the United States finally recognized Obregón's government, and Mexico might have come to terms with itself, had it not been for another round of armed rebellions.

In 1923, after he had served three years in office, with one to go, uprisings occurred in several states, and Obregón's forces nearly lost Mexico City.

Then the United States, not wanting more years of revolution, came to the rescue with arms and aircraft. One of the would-be presidential hopefuls escaped to California, where he earned his living as a singing teacher.

Even after the uprisings, Obregón might have survived if he had retained his realism, if his eyes had not grown bigger than the constitution he professed to uphold. He was entitled to one four-year term. As a successor he chose Plutarco Elias Calles, a man who did not live up to the nobility of his name. Wanting to return to the presidency, Obregón had the constitution rewritten to permit a non-sequential presidency and, after Calles'term, stood for re-election.

He was voted in. Three weeks later he was shot dead in a public restaurant by a portrait artist who belonged, it was said, to a group of fanatics offended by his attitude to the Church.

Obregón had been a popular president; had he not been so ambitious his realism might have carried him through. He was clear-eyed enough, however, not to have the arm he lost fighting against Pancho Villa disinterred and reburied with full military honours. He was no Santa Anna.

Plutarco Elias Calles, who again followed him into power, but not into office, was also a realist – he learnt from the mistake that Obregón had made. He controlled Mexican politics through others. He got rid of opponents by intrigue and murder. When he was finally bundled out of the country and sent to the United States, there were few Mexicans who regretted his departure.

But he left a mould that has never been broken. He founded the political party that governs Mexico today.

Alfredo Ramos Martínez (1872–1946): 'The Lady Colonel'; 'Zapata'; 'Genovevo de la O'.

Visions and Reality

The Revolution's Legacy

'Between the idea and the reality, between the motion and the act, falls the shadow' says T. S. Eliot in his poem, The Hollow Men. And so often this clear-eyed truth can be applied to Mexico.

In 1910 the country was stirred into revolution by the publication of Francisco Madero's book criticizing the dictatorship of Porfirio Díaz. It is a work that does not rank high in Mexican literature, but its ideas changed the course of history. Yet when Madero himself became president, he did little to bring reality to the dreams he had spun. Emiliano Zapata issued his Plan of Ayala, calling for the return to Mexican hands of all foreign-owned lands, for the breaking up of the large haciendas. Yet the only time he spent in Mexico City was a brief, almost furtive, few days. Then he scurried away from the seat of power, back to his security in the mountains of Morelos.

Venustiano Carranza, pictured as a saviour after the signing of his revolutionary constitution of 1917, who provided the basis for Mexican law today, whose views have been called the most important in the history of the revolution, took more from the people than he ever gave.

But if the men proved frail, what they said and did, how they lived and fought, inspired visions in others. The revolution's deeds, painted in glowing colours, spring from the muralists' walls. There, shining eyes see a golden future. From this have come some superb paintings.

Gonzaléz Camarena's biblical portrayal of Carranza with his pen in hand, signing the revolutionary document, is a powerful image of a country on the move. From the feathers of the symbolic eagle in the background come the faces of the legislators; from the Moses-like Carranza come the tablets of the law. It is inspiring; it has given heart to many.

Diego Rivera, Mexico's best-known painter, who lived through the revolution, saw the protagonists in shades of political extremes. In his mural of Emiliano Zapata in the Cortés Palace in Cuernavaca, the leader from Morelos is innocence and light. He wears the loose white clothing of a peasant; beside him a snow-white horse. In his hand is a sickle, lightly stained with the blood of the soldier at his feet. There is not a rifle in sight. Rivera's treatment of foreign investors in 'Night of the Rich', a mural in the Ministry of Education, Mexico City, is much more savage. The faces of John D. Rockefeller, J. P. Morgan and Henry Ford are hard, twisted with greed and avarice. On the table before them, there is only a thin yellow snake of ticker-tape; in the background is a safe. Diego Rivera was a Marxist, so his blacks and whites are more distinct than most.

Writers have seen Mexico's past a little more clearly, although their work is often romantically bent – especially that of foreigners. Graham Greene's *The Power and the Glory*, based on the anti-clerical campaign of President Calles in the early 1930s, when the total number of priests in Mexico was reduced to less than two hundred, has characters that are simply allegorical: the good-but-frail priest; the would-be good but bound-by-the-law army officer; the Judas character.

Perhaps the best novel of the revolution is Carlos Fuentes' *The Death of Artemio Cruz*. The protagonist, Artemio Cruz, on his deathbed recalls his years as a young soldier, how he fought with an idealism he lost after the war, becoming, as did so many in the Obregón years, a man who took what he could.

Yet out of the chaos, the corruption of ideals, the turning away from something better to an age-old practice of piracy, came the Mexico of today. The Institutional Revolutionary Party, known just as the PRI, which grew directly from the base established by President Calles in 1928, has never lost power. Now that the Soviet Union no longer exists, the PRI has become the

200. *The Angel stands atop the Monument to Independence in Mexico City, erected in 1910, one hundred years after the movement for freedom from Spain began. The figure dominates the Paseo de la Reforma, the city's central avenue, at the Zona Rosa. In the 1957 earthquake, the Angel crashed to the ground, but was undamaged. Her survival was seen by many as divine intervention.*

201. *Juan O'Gorman's fine mural representing Mexico's independence on the wall of Chapultepec Castle. Hidalgo, father of the independence movement, can be seen on the right, issuing his famous cry for freedom. O'Gorman spent two years perfecting this work, which he considered to be his most important achievement. (pp. 210-211)*

longest ruling party in the world today. Its grip on the country is firm. The memory of the revolution is too strong to allow any unbending of its rules. There is talk of change, there have been some token gestures, but not enough to permit real opposition. The party is the state. Membership is obligatory for anyone holding any office of any importance; in fact, no one is likely to be given even the lightest reins of power if not a member of the PRI in the first place. Generals, judges, police chiefs, all belong to it, as do union leaders. Unions themselves have a block-membership of the party, union contributions help finance it. The president picks his successor through a process that cannot readily be called democratic. The president listens to business leaders, newspaper owners, television chiefs, but in the end the decision is his. And when named, the PRI presidential candidate campaigns throughout the country as if his career depended on it, although so far no PRI candidate has ever lost the race.

Mexico's current president, Carlos Salinas de Gortari, came close. In 1988 he made it with just fifty-one per cent of the vote. As usual there were cries of fraud and vote-rigging by opposition parties, but these parties themselves depend on the government for their campaign funds.

Perhaps Salinas' narrow margin made him think. By PRI standards, he has proved remarkably liberal, perhaps realizing he has to be. Eighty per cent of Mexicans today are under forty years old and remember nothing of the revolution. To them Emiliano Zapata is no closer than a character played by Marlon Brando on the screen. They want a Mexico that is moving into the next century, a land that is not another violent Latin American country south of the U.S. border. They are looking for fresh hope.

President Salinas may start to give it to them. Already he has begun to bend one of the revolution's fundamental principles – the reorganizing of *ejido* lands. There are some twenty-eight thousand *ejido* farms worked by *campesinos,* most of whom were allotted their *ejidos* during the presidency of Lázaro Cárdenas (1934 to 1940). Cárdenas has been called the last true president of the Mexican people. He was the man who nationalized all foreign oil holdings. He was the man, many believe, who gave Mexico back to the Mexicans. So, is the current president tampering with a fundamental, popular belief when he begins to alter the *ejido* law, the law that permits such land to be inherited, but not sold or mortgaged? When he puts through Congress a motion that would permit such sales or mortgages, even to foreign companies, even to those who have been thought of for so long as the imperialist barons north of the U.S.-Mexican border, waiting for their chance to pounce on the wealth that is still in Mexico – is President Salinas de Gortari taking absurd risks?

He does not think so. He knows the system is not working. Mexico has to import grain and beans, powdered milk and other basic foodstuffs. A U.S. farmer produces nearly five times more than his Mexican counterpart. Something had to be done. Even Zapata's son, Mateo, now seventy-four, agrees that the *campesino's* right to do what he will with his land is a freedom that has long been wanting. 'This is the last step of the revolution,' Mateo Zapata has recently been quoted as saying.

Trouble with the Neighbours

Throughout its history Mexico has been subject to plunder. This is the umbilical cord that ties the past to the living present. From the time of the Elephant Man of Tepexpan, down through the Aztecs, the Maya, the conquistadores themselves, those who possessed have had their treasures

212. Diego Rivera (1886-1957),
Mexico's best-known artist, saw the
arrival of Hernán Cortés as the precursor
of disaster for the Indian race. His
murals, such as this one on the opposite
page, often contain searing criticism of
the Spaniards, who brought with them
slavery, disease and destruction.

213, 214. Tenochtitlán before the
conquistadores arrived. Seen here
through the eyes of Diego Rivera, it was a
place of broad avenues and majestic
temples. These scenes are part of the
gallery of murals Diego painted on the
walls of Mexico City's Presidential
Palace.

215. *The world-famous face of UNAM, the University of Mexico, in the south of Mexico City. Its ten-storey library was designed by Juan O'Gorman, the eminent Mexican architect and muralist. It highlights the country's past in mosaics that reflect Indian myth and legend. The University itself was founded in 1551.*

216, 217. *Native themes, Indian deities, symbols of ancient faiths, live on in modern Mexico. Entrances are often adorned with floral motifs from pre-Hispanic times. The fountain in Chapultepec Park, designed by Diego Rivera, was inspired by Indian representations of Tláloc, the water god.*

218, 219. Mexico is famous as a land of astonishing buildings. Much modern architecture with its geometrical lines is far closer to the pre-Hispanic monuments than to the curvacious Baroque of the colonial age. The severity of line is here relieved by use of brilliant colour, again in the national tradition, in the Camino Real Hotel and in the house of the Gilardi family, designed by Luis Barragán, both in Mexico D.F.

220. Mexico City, the metropolis with more inhabitants than any other in the world, a city of soaring buildings, throbbing excitement, and its fair share of traffic jams. Amongst it all, like the beetles they are, yellow Volkswagen taxis scurry to and fro. (pp. 226-227)

221. Taxco, the silver town, knitted into the hillside. Twisting streets lead up to the magnificent rose-coloured church of Santa Prisca. From Taxco came the first silver the conquistadores shipped back to Spain (pp. 228-229)

222. Night on the Pacific Coast: Acapulco, playground of the rich, where luxury hotels line the splendid shore. Tourism is a big business in Mexico, and nowhere bigger than in Acapulco, with its year-round sunshine and warm blue sea. (pp. 230-231)

223-228. A gallery of Mexican faces, old and young, solemn and smiling. Most Mexicans have a mixture of Indian and European blood. All are equal: no census has referred to racial origins since the 1940s. The girls, above right, are Mennonites from Zacatecas.

229, 230. *Whether dressed simply for work, top left, or elaborately for a religious festival, right, Mexicans wear their clothes with style and a certain natural grace.*

231. *An old lady with the traditional shawl, the rebozo, which protects from sun and rain, and can be used to carry goods.*

232. *Preparing young, tender cactus leaf for the cookpot. The spines are trimmed, the leaf is sliced, stir-fried and then served with tortillas.*

233, 234. Dignity and power are conveyed by the façade of these seats of government: the Municipal Palace at Tlaxcala, above, and the Presidential Palace on Zocalo Square in Mexico City.

235. Guadalajara, Mexico's second city, is a densely populated centre where graceful colonial arcades, ancient plazas and tree-shaded parks stand beside factories, supermarkets and parking lots. In 1991, a violent gas explosion tore apart much of the Reforma district, causing heavy loss of life and damage estimated in the region of 300 million dollars.

236. A courtyard in Querétaro, some
120 miles north of Mexico City. This
attractive town has some of the most
stylish architecture in the whole of the
country. It was in Querétaro that the last
emperor of Mexico, the ill-fated
Maximilian Hapsburg, was tried, found
guilty, and shot.

237. Mexican architectural styles have produced a curious cocktail in some places. Here, in Etzatlan, Jalisco, opposite page, the long, straight streets are as the Aztecs might have laid them down. The jumble of modern rooftops, however, would not have gladdened an ancient builder's eye.

238, 239. More successful are the works of Church and State. These examples, a church in Cholula, above, and the Museo de las Culturas in Mexico City, show greater architectural ambition.

wrested from them. In this respect, no one has been more guilty than the North American neighbours.

The United States took not only gold and silver, oil, fruit and sugar, it also took half of Mexico's land in a war where, in the end, boy heroes fought and lost against seasoned men. When the peace was signed, a token sum was paid, old debts were forgiven, but the land was lost.

It has been argued that the outcome of the revolution depended on which side the U.S. favoured at the time, which side was more likely to protect the interest of big business. Arms from North America went to the dictator Huerta, in the belief they might put an end to the more politically unreliable elements, in the eyes of the U.S.A., like Zapata, Villa and Carranza. Then President Wilson changed his mind, Villa was allowed to buy arms, and finally a huge arsenal was handed to Carranza in Veracruz. There was even talk by American power-lords of intervening in the revolution, of annexing Mexico as a whole. But the U.S. hesitated at so vast a step. So the arsenal was given to Carranza, and Zapata and Villa were lost.

Later, when Obregón was threatened, the Americans came in with massive assistance; this time aircraft were included. Obregón was a good guy in their book. There has never been a time, in all its independent existence, when the United States has not poked its finger deep into Mexican affairs. And Mexico's reaction has been hard and permanent. Schoolbooks today portray much of U.S. thinking as capitalistic and grasping. Not quite an Evil Empire, but not very far removed. However, American arms are part of the Mexican reality: piles of useless weapons are sold in markets; there are many proud owners of coffee tables allegedly made from the doors of haciendas in the north, Pancho Villa country, with bullets in them – evidence, it is said, of executions at the time of the revolution. Of course, there may be a small, quiet industry producing doors with lead in them, but the fascination survives.

Emilio Fernández, the fine actor and film director, spent time in jail for shooting a man during an argument over the making of a movie. The incident happened on location, Fernández was in costume, the gun he was acting with was not a prop, the bullets were real. 'El Indio', as he was popularly called, settled the matter according to an old-established scenario. The weapon was at hand. He used it – with deadly effect.

This trait, this resistance to pressure, is very basic to Mexican character. The gringos, the big-boys, the people who have come to give orders and to take, are stubbornly confronted. Those who ask politely, who treat a proud people with the respect they deserve, are often given everything they need – and a great deal more besides.

Mexicans frequently refer to Americans as gringos. Some think the word may have come from the song 'Green grow the rushes, oh,' sung by Irish volunteers who flocked to support Simon Bolivar in his liberation of the South American countries from Spanish colonial hold. It was alleged to be their marching song. What seems more likely is that it comes from an old Spanish word meaning gibberish, double-Dutch, which was applied particularly to North Americans as the foreigners most often encountered south of the Rio Grande.

But what interests Mexicans of today more, with their eighty pet cent of population below the age of forty and their twenty-five per cent, and rising, middle class, is not what the United States is likely to take away but what it can supply. Cablevision feeds into Mexico. U.S. soap operas, the sagas of the rich and famous, TV movies, are seen in a great number of Mexican homes. If women's skirts get shorter in New York, the hem-line will be lifted in

240. Once-conflicting cultures have fused in many ways. The Spanish clergy accepted Indian touches of colour and decoration when building churches. The Indians welcomed the livestock that came with the conquistadores. Horses and cattle were unknown until the Spaniards came, as was the wheel's use for transport.

Mexico City. If men's jackets are baggier in Los Angeles, they will hang out in the discotheques in the heart of Mexico. If the latest trends in Miami or Chicago are towards New Era, Heavy Metal or Rap, they will be echoed throughout Mexico, perhaps in versions a little sharper, louder and less tuned to the western ear.

Films are popular in Mexico and cinemas well attended. They fall into two major groups: foreign films shown in original-language versions and Mexican-made films in Spanish. Foreign films are subtitled but not dubbed: the thinking behind this was to protect Mexican movie-making. It was recognized that in a country with a high illiteracy rate, slow-readers or non-readers were unlikely to struggle through a movie in a *gringo* tongue. This has proved to be largely the case. Foreign films do quite well in Mexico City, but the smaller towns, the *pueblos*, favour the local product: comedies with well-worn plots, westerns with lots of blood and violence, and at times good social dramas set in tenements or slum areas, in which the raw side of Mexican life is treated with a hard-eyed realism, and a humour that levels everything.

In the same mould, but softer, often sweeter, are the numerous telenovelas, the TV series, that run on and on. With titles like *Burning Passions* or *The Rich Also Cry*, they are enormously successful and have been exported to Spain as well as other Latin American countries. Like the film comedies, their plots are used again and again, at times with the same actors in similar parts in different series. They are made with a degree of professional expertise that is astounding, considering that quite likely there has been no real rehearsal. Up to four half-hour episodes may be shot in a day. The actors are given a script, shown the basic moves, and a prompt advises them of their next line – through an ear receiver – while they are listening to the words of others in the scene.

We had a maid called Carmen, a stocky little realist with coffee-coloured skin and a long black pig-tail that was always shining, as was her smile. She had been married for seven years and so had seven children. After the seventh, her husband went to live with his other wife in another part of the city. She never saw him again, had no more children, and was not really surprised at his going. The second house, second family, is not uncommon with Mexican men. Eventually they abandon one for the other, but usually after the children have grown. Mexican men seem to think they are proving themselves when their women give birth, yet they are sentimentally fond of children and cannot bear to leave them. Whether this is part of the much talked about *machismo* or not is hard do say. *Macho,* in Spanish, simply means male. *Machismo* is a convenient word to express all the selfish motives of men, but there is nothing particularly Mexican about that – the Englishman in his club, the American in his lodge, is part of the same breed.

As far as Carmen was concerned, her husband's departure was a relief. It freed her to live her own life, however difficult. She had a black-and-white TV set in the house she was in the process of building – both were the stuff that her dreams were made of. The house was a breech-block construction with a dirt floor and holes in the walls covered with curtain, since glazed windows were beyond her means.

She worked to bring up her seven children, who went to local schools. She always had a cat or dog as a household pet. They always seemed to die. Yet nothing ever depressed her, bent her spirit. She worked in three other houses near where we lived. Each day she spent four hours on a bus travelling to and fro. My wife, Virginia, visited her when she went into hospital for a hernia operation. Carmen's face was the same sickly colour as the pale green hospital wall, but she got over that too.

Nineteenth-century lady watches the world go by.

Carmen became a friend; she still writes from time to time – her children taught her how. When we left, she wanted to buy everything we had that had been made abroad, especially in the U.S.A. We gave her what she wanted, little treasures that sit in her windowless house surrounded by her courage.

Carmen survives, she and her children will endure, they are carried by a belief in themselves and something deeper, a mixture of what is Catholic and the undying hue of folklore that belongs to an ancient faith, that flows deeper in the blood – their own sense of the need to suffer. To suffer, many are convinced, is the reason for their being in this world.

Bearing the Cross

A man died on the cross in Mexico City not so very long ago. One Easter, during a re-enactment of the Crucifixion, one of the many that take place all over Mexico, a young man carried a cross on his back, was whipped, scourged and finally bound to it in the crucifix position. Left there too long, he died, possibly of suffocation. His struggling would have been seen as part of the performance: he had been carefully chosen for the part, had rehearsed, and was proud to have been selected.

His death was another manifestation of the rawness that often goes hand in hand with religion. In Mexico ninety per cent of the population claim to be Catholic. Other religions have only a tiny voice. Priests came to the country with the Spanish conquistadores; others followed. The new religion was laid heavily over a pagan past. The native peoples were overcome, so were their savage gods, the gods who demanded blood and sacrifice. And after the idols were broken, when their shards lay on the ground, a Spanish church was built over the Indian temple and the spirits of the old and the new, in the eyes of many, became fused. Indian chants were turned into Catholic hymns; part of the savage spirit survived.

And then, in 1531, a miracle occurred that all of Mexico acknowledges. On a pagan site, the former temple of the Aztec earth goddess Tonantzín, an image of the Virgin Mother appeared before an Indian convert to Christianity, Juan Diego. Hearing his name being called, he turned to see a dark-haired, dark-skinned Madonna wearing a long white robe embroidered with gold. She told Juan Diego that she wanted a shrine to be built in her name on the hilltop where she stood. She then caused roses to bloom from the barren earth to prove she was no illusion.

Juan Diego took the roses to the Bishop of Mexico. They left the figure of the Virgin on the serape he wore that remains there today, high above the altar in the shrine erected in the Virgin's name. The Virgin of Guadalupe, as she is known, is Mexico's patron saint. She turned the tide toward Christianity. She made it simple for any doubting Indian to embrace the old earth goddess in a new and radiant form.

Every December 12, the anniversary of Juan Diego's vision, Mexicans make their pilgrimages to the basilica of the Virgin of Guadalupe, built on the ancient site of the goddess Tonantzín. During the year, at times of sickness or disaster, they have prayed to the Virgin for help, to ease their suffering, to erase their pain. If they feel their prayers have been answered, they pay the penances they have pledged. Most often this involves walking a certain distance to the basilica on their knees, along asphalt and concrete roadway, up the twisting stairway to the shrine on the top of the hill. When their knees become bloody, they wrap them in bandages, which become quickly stained. There are Boy Scouts to help them on their journey, and some of them make it to the top. They have suffered, they have borne their suffering, they have demonstrated the depth of their faith.

All this has been positive for the Catholic Church in Mexico. On the negative side the vision has not been nearly as bright. After Mexico became independent, after the last Spanish viceroy had gone, those in power turned against the Church, objecting to its privileges, the amount of property that was in ecclesiastical hands, the fact that priests were outside civil law: they could only be tried by ecclesiastical courts.

Benito Juárez, Mexico's first and only Indian president, held a life-long hatred for the Church. After his time, the laws he laid down, although not erased from the statute books, were less stringently enforced until the revolution, then the hatred blazed afresh. And when the revolution was over, when Obregón had bought peace by simply calculating what each man was worth, when Calles was the power on or behind the presidential throne, then the Church was truly ground into the earth.

In 1926 Plutarco Elias Calles launched an attack on the Church that was the most serious ever sustained by Catholicism in all its long, and at times tortured, Mexican history. The reaction that followed was like some medieval contest between Pope and King. A great number of foreign-born clergymen were deported, what Catholic schools remained were closed, Mexican-born priests were subject to registration and were ordered to leave their churches and to abstain from administering the sacraments. The Catholic protest was immense. A League for the Defence of Religious Liberty was formed, financed by wealthy Catholics, many of them Americans. Boycotts were called for; people were asked to refrain from purchasing petroleum products and, something dear to every Mexican's heart, lottery tickets.

But, in effect, the League's methods were much more violent than that. Armed bands of Catholic guerrillas attacked local government officials. Village schoolmasters were made special targets because of their liberal ideas,

Famous photograph of Pancho Villa (smiling) and Emiliano Zapata.

their often-expressed contempt for religion. The Catholic guerrillas became known as the *Cristeros* – from their rallying cry: *'Viva Cristo Rey'* 'Long live Christ the King'. Photographs of them show groups with rifles, pistols and that symbol of almost every Mexican outlaw – the crossed bandoliers, shiny with bullets, one over each proud shoulder.

Government reaction was swift and brutal. Callista generals let their armies loose in the countryside. *Cristero* guerrillas were shot, tortured and burned. Their bodies were strung from telegraph poles beside the railways, so no traveller would be in any doubt about the ferocity of reprisal for opposing the anti-clerical law. Churches were demolished, congregations were shot *en masse*. When President Obregón, elected for a second term, was shot in a restaurant by Toral, a Catholic who was said to be acting on his own, the brutality against the *Cristeros* was increased. In some states the Church was virtually eliminated. Then the pressure was eased; greed, the scramble for power, pushed the anti-Catholic force aside.

Slowly the Catholic Church in Mexico, and the others who follow in its wake, have returned to their rightful place. When the well-respected Lázaro Cárdenas became president in 1934, the situation eased. Although no friend of the Church, Cárdenas left it in relative peace. President Manuel Avila Camacho, in office from 1940 to 1946, confessed to being a believer. But the anti-clerical laws remained on the statute books. Priests and nuns were not allowed to wear their clerical robes in public – any seen in the streets, until very recently, were tourists taking a holiday. And, most significantly, no public Masses were permitted.

But that law was quietly brushed aside when Pope John Paul II came to visit. The Pope held several open-air Masses, on both his visits, and no government official made any attempt to prevent them. They were hugely, overwhelmingly attended, as are most other church functions – which shows what the Mexican people really want. Although church weddings were not recognized officially until very recently, most Mexicans who could afford it had two ceremonies; the state one to abide by the law, the church one where the real celebrations took place.

And now, after something like seventy-five years, that is, since the 1917 Constitution, or nearly one hundred and forty if we look back to the laws enacted after independence, the Mexican government has finally come to recognize what the people want in terms of religious freedom. The Pope's visits must have had something to do with this change of legislative heart; the fact that the current president, Carlos Salinas de Gortari, is seeking wider popular support could also have contributed to the legalizing of Mexico's religious organizations. Whatever put an end to the battle between Church and State, a new beginning is now in sight. In 1991 Congress passed constitutional amendments that will permit members of the clergy to vote in elections, to wear their habits in the street, and run religious schools.

Mexico appears determined to make real changes to the way the country is run in this last decade of the twentieth cenntury. Industries, banks and companies that were nationalized, some as recently as the 1970s, are being sold back to the private sector. Foreign investment is being encouraged again. But the reform that may mean most to the Mexican people is that affecting the anti-clerical laws. In most small towns and villages, in Mexico as elsewhere, in spite of legislation the Church has been at the heart of the community. Catholicism, and other religions, have never been dead in Mexico; they have merely been outside the law. In Mexican eyes this has not lessened them, for this is a country with a spirit that defies authority, it is the spirit that has made the people what they are.

The Mexican Way

The Showmen

They dive from cliffs, a hundred feet high, into a narrow curling wave. They spin from a giant pole, tied by their feet, until their heads touch the ground. They dress like electric cowboys, all glitter and silver and gold, sombreros the size of tables, and prance their bloodline steeds. They put on the robes of Martians and wrestle in a ring. These are just some of the many Mexicans displaying themselves, their history, the showmanship that flows in their blood.

They come from every part of Mexico, from nearly every walk of life. Some are rich, some have practically nothing at all, but all share the need to parade themselves before their fellows, before an audience that knows it sees part of itself in this performance.

It goes back in time to the lordly Maya with their resplendent quetzal feathers of brilliant green, their jaguar cloaks of fawn, of chocolate brown. It is part of the Aztec ceremony where black-clad priests cut the blood-red heart out of sacrificial victims painted blue. It coils down toward today through passageways of churches, cathedrals, rooms where prayers were heard, adorned with the figure of Christ hanging from a cross, decorated with the vivid colours of a pagan past. It is as recent as the latest Hollywood spectacle, the last-played telenovela. And with it ride the sounds of laughter and of prayer, the gasps of fear and the sighs of adoration, the thunder of applause.

Perhaps its most ancient manifestation is seen in a performance based on the Totonac rain dance. It is a show that now takes place on a daily basis, if the audience is large enough, although it was previously only performed on Corpus Christi. Instead of the consecrated Host being carried through the streets, Indian dancers in native dress, long coloured streamers swirling from their skull caps, spin from a pole in ever-increasing circles until they reach the earth. In times past the pole-tree was searched for yearly, gifts were laid before its base the night before it was felled, in ceremonies not unlike the Maya blessing their ball courts before the game. Now the pole is permanently in place.

The pole spinners perform at El Tajín near Papantla in the state of Veracruz, where the ruins of tenth-century temples are scattered about. There is also a ball court amongst the half-ruined temples, but no ceremonies are held there today. The spinners are hard-faced, hard-bodied little men with oriental eyes and, more often than not, an expensive gold watch on their wrist. They climb, they wind their ropes about a circling platform, and when ready, they descend. Then their impassive faces open into smiles as gasps turn into applause and their rewards are collected in a basket brimming with peso notes.

As impressive, but descending through a different branch, are the *charros* – the electric horsemen and women who, dressed like elaborate cowboys, spin horses, rope cattle, lift their wide sombreros and shout their excitement aloud. Their background lies much further north than Veracruz, in the hard flayed country of the massive border states where haciendas spread for miles, where Pancho Villa and his bandits rode, yelling their cries of freedom, taking what they could. The *charros* wear narrow trousers, adorned with silver links, thick silver-studded belts, embroidered shirts and short jackets, quite often smothered in gold. They may look as if they have stepped out of a poster for a circus, but their horsemanship is superb. And the women, in their brightly-coloured ruffled dresses, are equally skilled performers. As are those who entertain the crowd with their *rancheras,* their cowboy songs, guitars and voices lifted in rousing country tunes, all more or less the same, all invigorating. Around, invading, everywhere are the smells of roasting

Portrait of the celebrated poet Carlos de Siguenza y Góngora (1645–1700).

meats, the mealy odour of tortillas. The audience consists of those who have come to watch and those who have come to wonder – boys sitting on the railings, knowing that one day they will have their turn.

Lower still in heritage, their roots going back no further than the recent past, are the wrestlers, those who perform in *lucha libre*, the ceremonial free-for-all. Also lower on the economic scale is the audience that comes to shout, to scream, to throw its plastic beer cups if displeased. Those who get into the ring to display themselves, to roll and jump, to grunt and groan, range from midgets to gaints, from lean, fit men to ageing barrels of muscle and fat. Lycra seems to be their favourite fabric, the shinier the better. Many are masked, close-fitted with headgear that must make breathing difficult and sweating a torment, a real hazard in a not very dangerous game. Some arrive oiled and shining, each muscle carefully displayed, others are dressed like creatures from a distant planet, like gods from another time.

While pop-music blasts, amidst tumultuous shouting, the audience bets with whoever will take an offer, money furiously changes hands, is held for a while, then resumes its course. Wrestling similar to this occurs in many countries, but there is something about the Mexican version that makes for greater flamboyance, that gets deeper beneath the skin. Hulk Hogan might thrash them all but not come nearly as close to the audience's heart as a flying midget dressed like a future god.

And further down the scale, remote from the spinning Totonac rain dancers, from the rich *charros* and their expensive steeds, more basic than the wrestlers in their masks of sweat, are those who perform at traffic lights. On this low rung of the entertainment ladder are the conjurors, the jugglers, the fire-eaters who, for the few moments between red and green, hold an audience captive.

The conjurors and jugglers spin balls and oranges, hoops and coloured clubs, anything they can lay their dextrous hands on. In the few brief moments, while impatient feet wait to press the accelerator, they make silver trinkets shine and disappear, flash again and return from behing a reluctant driver's ear, then hold out a palm for reward. Some have painted faces, suits of clowns, look like the Marx brothers or Charlie Chaplin, mime like Marcel Marceau. They work at a frenzied pace, smiling, laughing, entertaining, hoping for cash, for enough to eat, for money to buy make-up. But in their hearts they hope for more – applause, a split-second of glory. It must be this that spurs them. Others, their faces impassive, with no twitch of movement, no hint of a smile, also hold out their hands to beg in doorways, to ask at sidewalk tables. They have none of the spirit of the traffic-light clowns, none of the sense of showmanship, of irrepressible display.

And with the clowns and jugglers, sharing the same exhaust-fume arena, are the fire-eaters. They are close to the bed-rock at the bottom of the pole. *Tragafuegos,* the Mexicans call them, swallowers of fire. They fill their mouths with kerosene and blow it at a flame. A great orange burst shoots from their lips – they are most effective at night. A dramatic explosion leaps from them, it is their call to be seen and applauded, it is their desperate cry to be centre-stage. Desperate and, in the end, deadly. They develop mouth ulcers, their teeth fall out, the explosive liquids that leap from the lips begin to erode their brain. Yet they continue, driven by the same harsh Muse.

Far to the south, where the Pacific wind blows softly, high on a cliff face, the only traffic a swirling bird, the divers of Acapulco are impelled by the same basic urge; to be watched, however briefly, to do what so few dare. Their audience is not captive; it comes of its own accord. The divers, for years members of the same family, throw themselves gracefully out into the

241. Deep in the south of Yucatán, near the border with Belize, are the early 'classic' ruins of Kohunlich, AD 250-500. Here, outside the Temple of the Masks, walls of high-nosed, full-lipped Mayan faces stare out across the void of time.

air and curve downward into a narrow cove where the sea beats in. These men are athletes, their timing is perfect. They catch the wave when it is full, when the water is deepest. The diver goes down into the whitewashed blue, and a minute later reappears and signals to the crowd above. The gasps turn into a clamour, for that moment it is his. Payment is made, valour is rewarded, perhaps the least of it is cash.

There are many who perform with no regard for financial gain, simply for the love of display. At parties, fiestas, Mexico's equivalent of carnival, the people emerge, elaborately dressed, to dance and sing, to give free vent to their love of display. They wear colourful robes, feathered head-dresses in reds and greens, yellows, oranges and bright blues. Indian costumes, going back beyond the Spaniards and the Catholicism they brought, accompany those who march on their knees on the day of the Virgin of Guadalupe paying homage to the Mother of Christ. It seems that always, everywhere you turn, there is a spectacle, a re-flowering of time-past and time-present, that springs from the Mexican soul, a re-enactment of the power of the gods that ruled and those that came to replace them.

There are other activities with some of the same vitality, but they are not quite part of the blood. Bullfighting, a Spanish graft, has its season in Mexico. Some of it is spirited, but it is not a Mexican feast. It is an adopted form of ritual killing that had no place in the Indian past. Soccer is immensely popular, arousing intense passions, though Mexico has not produced one of the world's great teams. The only Olympic medalist from Mexico in recent years has been a solitary long-distance walker, a man on his own with the knowledge of how to survive the journey, a man applauded, purely and simply, for what he has done bravely on his own.

The Fixers
Sacred and Profane

There is a lot of magic in Mexico; it is something else that runs deep in the blood. There are beliefs and practices in every social level that go back to when Mexican time began.

When I was working on my novel, *The Fire Cloud*, I asked a friend in Mexico City if it would be unreal to invent a witch, a *bruja,* whom my fictional Mexican president consulted about what the future might hold. The friend replied: 'Of course not. As a matter of fact, I know the *bruja* the current president consults. She's a friend of mine.'

In a country where ninety per cent of the people claim to be Catholic, the number of witches, *curanderas* – those who heal with herbs and lotions – and sorceresses is surprisingly high. These are usually women, although their male counterparts exist. They may be old or young, wrinkled or smooth-faced, and are always known as Doña – Maria, Chona or Guadalupe, whatever their Christian name may be. Doña, the equivalent of Madam, is a title of honour and respect. And respected they are.

They follow practices that have never died, never been erased by over-taking cultures. And many of them are surprisingly universal. Their curative, magical, influential talents are applied in two directions: to rid a victim of pain, fear or disease, and to turn the mind of a lover, a potential benefactor or someone who might menace. What they use in their efforts to achieve their minor miracles, the ingredients, the processes, the ceremonies, are also spread around the world. Hair, toenails, fingernails, those odd body tissues that continue to grow for a little while after death and, consequently, are

242. Carved from a single block of basalt weighing almost 20 tons, this giant head is one of many left by the Olmecs in the swampland of La Venta, among the coastal mangroves of Tabasco state. The Olmecs, called the first civilized peoples of Middle America, spread a culture that influenced all others that followed.

243. The basalt from which this massive head was carved was brought to the site from some 60 miles away. Today the heads have been moved again: some to the National Museum of Anthropology, Mexico City, others to an open-air exhibition in Villahermosa, Yucatán. The only monuments in La Venta now are the giant oil rigs.

244. The Olmec head, with its curious helmet, has distinctly Mongol features. This is thought to indicate that the Olmec forefathers were part of a wave of Asian migrants that came across the Bering Strait and down through North America.

251

245. *Teotihuacán, the remains of a once magnificent city. In its prime, about AD 100, Teotihuacán knew enormous wealth, beauty and power. Wide avenues formed the city's grid, stately buildings lined the huge plazas, where citizens held markets, danced, strolled in conversation. Now Teotihuacán is a city of ghosts.*

246, 247. Each detail of Teotihuacán was carefully planned. The themes that adorn the pyramids, the serpent's heads with their flowing plumes, the repeated, circular, all-seeing eye, the layered staircases, were fitted together to produce a majestic whole. The mighty Aztecs, who found the city in ruins, thought Teotihuacán had been the dwelling place of gods older than their own, and respected the site as holy land.

248. *The Temple of the Warriors at Chichén Itzá, above, where a square mile of scrub forest has been cleared to reveal a magnificent blending of Toltec and Maya architecture.*

249. *Chichimec ruins at Teotenango in the Toluca valley.*

250. Dominating the landscape at Chichén Itzá is El Castillo, the pyramid of Kukulcán. Four flights of stairs, each with 91 steps, lead to the summit. Inside the pyramid is a sacred chamber where a red jaguar with eyes of jade and fangs of flint broods over the throne of long-gone priests.

251. More steps at the ruins of Malinalco, raised by the Aztecs.

252. Although much of Monte Albán
has been excavated and restored, a great
deal lies undiscovered. Here, a
partly-cleared temple overlooks the city
of Oaxaca. Other pyramids, some no
more than shaped and overgrown hills,
remain untouched, except by grave
robbers who have tunnelled inside and
carried off anything they could sell.

253, 254. *A huge stretch of flattened land, carved smooth by the Zapotecs, is the basis of Monte Albán, described as the greatest ceremonial site in all Mexico. Among the bas-relief figures found here are the Dancers, left, who show strong Olmec influence in their design and facial expressions.*

255, 256. *Kabah, where, at the Palace of Masks near Uxmal, the face of Chac, god of water, stares out repeatedly with round stone eyes. Some 600 images cover the classic Puuc façade.*

257-259. At Cacaxtla, near the old Indian town of Tlaxcala, an exciting new series of Maya-style frescoes was discovered in 1975. Scenes of fighting warriors, elaborately robed lords and priests, were revealed for the first time in centuries.

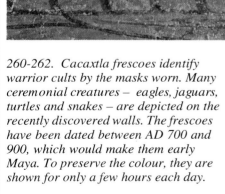

260-262. *Cacaxtla frescoes identify warrior cults by the masks worn. Many ceremonial creatures – eagles, jaguars, turtles and snakes – are depicted on the recently discovered walls. The frescoes have been dated between AD 700 and 900, which would make them early Maya. To preserve the colour, they are shown for only a few hours each day.*

263. In the valley of Toluca, west of Mexico City, lie the ruins of Teotenango, once a noble centre of Chichimec culture. Now all that remain are the uncovered skeletons of stately buildings, pyramids, stairs leading up to gracious courts.

264. Among the ruins of Teotenango are the remnants of ball courts where Chichimec players once sweated in the sun. Bitter matches were fought, for at times the loser forfeited his life. The sloping surface of one such court can be seen on the left.

265, 266. At Chichén Itzá, a Chac Mool waits at the end of an avenue of carved columns for the heart of a sacrificial victim to carry to the gods.

267., 268. At Tula, city of the Toltecs, these giant warriors guard the Temple of the Morning Star or Dawn. Dwarfing the men of today, as they did those who created them, these atlantes represent warriors wearing feather head-dresses, ear-plugs and breastplates. In one hand they carry a spear-thrower, in the other the short spears they hurled.

269. The Temple of the Morning Star at Tula, north-west of Mexico City, was once the impressive capital of the Toltec empire. These remarkable statues, about 20 feet in height, were raised to support a further layer of the pyramid, now lost.

270. The ruins of Monte Albán, ancient Zapotec capital. The Zapotecs were displaced by the Mixtecs, who overlaid the imperial site with their own distinctive contributions – craftwork in gold, silver and jade.

271, 272. At Palenque, a skull stares blindly from a wall, a warrior cries out from his bed of stone. This centre of worship of the Maya, in the heart of the Yucatán, lay undiscovered for centuries, entombed by the lush green jungle.

273. The Temple of Inscriptions, Palenque. In 1952, a magnificent tomb containing the remains of a Maya lord, surrounded by gold and jewelry, was discovered here. At the entrance of the crypt were the skeletons of the guards who had remained to protect him.

274, 275. *Maya architecture at its finest. The triumphal arch at Labná above, and the crumbling House of Doves at Uxmal are both part of the enormous, interlinked, ceremonial complex south of Mérida that flourished in the first millennium AD.*

276. *Uxmal's House of Nuns and Pyramid of the Dwarfs, once fine examples of Maya Puuc, Low Hills, architecture. Here, stone columns with an hour-glass shape supported thatch-roofed huts – cool places along the tropical coast.*

277. *The remains of El Tajín, Veracruz, formerly a major political centre with a vast complex of pyramids, avenues, palaces and ball courts. Now only semi-restored ruins and earth mounds can be seen.*

278. Honeycombed with layered entrances, this main pyramid at El Tajín was dedicated to Tláloc, the water god. It is known as Los Nichos, the Niches, because of the many apertures on all four sides of the ascending tiers.

279. Profile of a Toltec warrior, bas-relief on a column at the Temple of the Warriors, Chichén Itzá. Although it became a Maya city, strong Toltec influence is present in the architecture of Chichén Itzá. (p. 274)

280. Fierce, well-armed and deadly were the warriors the Spaniards encountered when they arrived to conquer New Spain. Though the force led by Cortés was ludicrously small, its weapons were superior to the obsidian-bladed axe the Indians carried. (p. 275)

281, 282. (pp. 278-279) A number of ancient tribes, among them the Maya, the Mixtecs, the Aztecs, inscribed the history of their race in picture-symbol books. Each codex was painted on bark paper or deer hide, and folded accordion-like to form a book. Vivid and descriptive, they show the past and everyday life of the people.

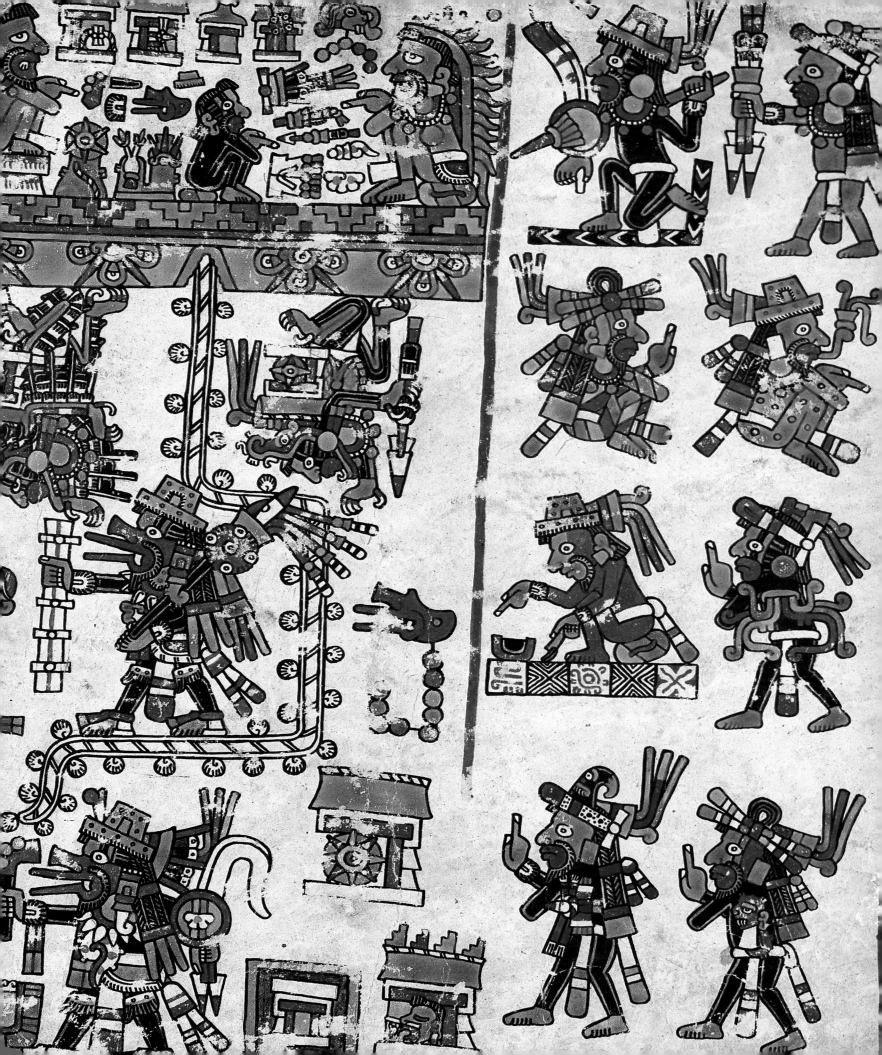

believed to contain the juice of life itself, are often employed. As they were in medieval England, as they are in the Fiji Islands where I was born.

An infinite range of plants and herbs, leaves and powdered barks are used by the magic-makers. Copal, a mixture of tree resins, is burned like incense, its heavy smoke giving potency to any ceremony. In practically any Mexican market there is a stall, a corner table, where herbs and potions, copal and shreds of bark are sold. On the night before the Day of the Dead, the rich smell of incense, mixed with the hot wax of a thousand candle-flames, fills the air in cemeteries all over Mexico. Families gather, to sit all night around the grave of a loved one, hoping to make some contact, however brief, with the spirits that have gone from this earth forever.

The Mexican Indian lived in a world of spirits, but this is not simply an ancient belief. No one knows how many Indians there are, how many are of mixed blood, how many carry a pure Spanish strain. Census information of this sort has not been collected for the last fifty years. What is beyond doubt, however, is the power of spiritual belief, the awareness of the closeness of death, the strength of its embracing arm. On the Day of the Dead, that night of watchfulness between the first and second of November, among the foods that are laid out on the gravesites, the favourite dishes of those who have gone before, are skulls made of coloured sugar, bright impertinences displayed to keep a brooding shadow at bay. They are eaten by laughing lips, but there is a touch of uncertainty in the level eyes.

This is, in part, a public display, shared with a hundred other families. More personal, humbler, are the consultations made with the *curanderas* face to face, when the problems are discussed in the quiet of a room, when the moments of magic enter. There is a fine line to be drawn between the *curanderas*, with herbal potions, and the *brujas*, with witch's powers.

When witches attempt to work their spells, when they need a tuft of hair, the parings from a lover's fingernails, they move away from herbs and leaves, and turn to eggs, live chickens and bark. Eggs are most important: hen eggs, turkey, duck, all seem to work. Their yolks have the power to absorb evil, to draw an illness, into their hidden core.

In matters of the heart the process is less bloody. When a woman wants to attract a man – and most of those who consult Mexican witches are women blessed or cursed by love – two bark-paper figures are cut, and the arms of the male are folded around the female. Thus bound, they are passed through the copal smoke from the incense burner, smoke is blown into the figures' mouths, then they are given to the woman. Now she needs a tuft of hair or a fingernail or two from the desired man. These are then tied to the male image with a thread of the woman's favourite colour. After that it is just a matter of waiting patiently, taking the figures to bed with her, feeding them a little of everything she eats and burning candles for them.

It is not recorded how effective the process has been throughout Mexico, but there are enough *brujas, curanderas* and the like in business to suggest a widespread practice.

Almost as old, certainly as basic, is the other common Mexican practice, the other way of fixing things. That is the bribe, the sweetening of the palm, the greasing of the wheels. An old Mexican said to me once: 'Oil is cheaper than steel.' And while, with a western upbringing, it is easy to criticize and condemn, this is the way the world has turned in Mexico for generations.

Alvaro Obregón, one of Mexico's best-loved presidents, put together the shattered remains of the country after the revolution, after civil wars had torn it apart, by calculating the price every former insurgent leader needed to

283. An Aztec manuscript, 'Mexico City', with the emblem of Mexico: an eagle on a cactus.

281

keep him quiet, to keep his guns at rest. Obregón dealt and bartered, paid, placated and gave, exchanged favours, stakes in industry, for prosperity and peace. And it worked. Slowly the country moved together, became what it is.

This is a process that goes back to the dawn of history. There has never been a time when gods or priests or overlords did not demand what they were due. The Mexican police, who wear powder-blue uniforms, are known sometimes as the *azules*, the blues. They are also known as the *mordelónes*, the biters, the takers of *mordidas*, bites or bribes.

I had a motorcycle in Mexico for a while, a bright green Honda 360, a beautiful machine. Riding it through Mexican traffic was an adventure in itself. One day a police sergeant on a similar bike drew up alongside me, asked me to pull over. It was the lunch-hour, a risky time in traffic – there is lunch-money to be 'earned'. The sergeant politely asked me for the Honda's papers, then looked at them doubtfully for a long time. In the end he told me they were not in order and that he would have to impound the bike.

I protested, he shrugged, flicked the papers and suggested we ride to the nearest *Delegacíon*, the nearest police station, and sort the matter out. Of course, he told me, once the bike is in the *Delegacíon* it will be awfully hard to get it out. What is more, it would cost a lot of money.

'How can this be fixed?' I asked, using the formula I had been told was almost magic in its effect. 'What can be done?'

The sergeant's smile grew. We were speaking the same language now. He came closer and suggested in a quieter voice that forty American dollars, or the equivalent in pesos, would put the matter right. He was almost apologetic, but he was sure I realized that this was the best way to settle things for both of us.

I paid him. We shook hands. Finally, when he had given me back my papers, I asked him what I had to do to put them in order, to make sure they were not questioned again. 'Señor,' he replied, 'leave forty dollars with them. You will never have another problem.' He then saluted and rode away.

That is how the system works on nearly every level. Oil is certainly cheaper than steel – and it causes no sparks to fly. In schools and government offices, in police stations and courts of law, the system of fixing matters with cash is accepted as part of life. For obvious reasons it is encountered most frequently among the police. They are out in the streets where the people are. This does not mean that the Mexican policeman is without a heart, but the kindness offered by a British bobby or the protection given by a New York Irish cop is not so common. From the point of view of the man in powder-blue accepting his hand-out, the reasoning is simple: if, in a country of grinding poverty, you are rich enough to own a car, a truck, a motorcycle, you can certainly afford to pay.

The police-bite is not applied to the same extent in poorer areas. Those who live in what are called the *ciudades perdidas,* the lost cities, in a jungle of dwellings made from anything that will protect them, from cinder blocks to flattened cans, have little money to pay the police, and often never see them. But they pay in another manner, also part of the Mexican system. They pay with their vote to the PRI, the political party in power. On election day their votes are carefully counted, sometimes more than once. In return, the electricity and water they are stealing from the metropolitan grid through a tangle of pipes and wires that bind them inextricably to the source of power will be legitimized. New cables and tubing will be installed, house titles will suddenly come through. So the people and the PRI continue, each in their own way, accepting that the system works for both.

Yet Mexico has ways of surprising. Out of the sombre shadows of the jungle will fly the brilliance of a bird, a scarlet macaw, perhaps, with its bands of red and yellow and blue, a bird that, incidentally, inhabits most parts of Mexico. It is an image that returns frequently in this country of bright and dark. On the highways, often miles from any town or city, are the *Angeles Verdes,* the Green Angels. These patrols sent out by the Department of Transport to help travellers certainly live up to their name.

They re-started my car for me once by the side of the road. I offered a tip, nothing more, to express my thanks. It was waved away with a smile. 'We are here to serve you,' one of them said. He was a man who spoke the truth. They, like the police, get only a minimum wage but their attitude springs from a different source. Like a child's drawing, they fill one with hope.

Frontispiece of a history of Campeche, first published in 1632.

A Moveable Feast

To end this tour in time and space, this look at Mexico's past and present, let us enjoy a feast of Mexican food. Like the country it is rich, tasty, succulent and often bites the tongue. When a dish is good, the Mexicans simply say, *Que rico!* How rich! It is a comment that expresses everything.

In the Ciudad del Carmen, on the Campeche coast, there is a bronze statue of a giant prawn, a creature that brought wealth to that part of the world, especially before the oil boom. Giant prawns, oysters, *ceviche* – that mixture of fish-flesh marinated in lime juice – with tomato, onion and fresh coriander, make up the dish we will start with. It is called *vuelve a la vida,* a return to life. It tastes of everything good in the sparkling sea and consuming it, you can definitely feel life returning.

To accompany it, I would recommend a glass of a good full-bodied red wine from Aguascalientes, in the high country north of Mexico City. These reds from Cabernet stock are robust enough to stand up to the competition they get from the food. Mexican white wines are best left alone, but Mexican lager-type beer is excellent. It can be, and is, drunk with everything. Tequila, as a side-shot, without the salt or lime, is a dangerous companion.

After the *vuelve a la vida,* now that the blood is flowing again, the world of the tortilla waits to be explored. Tortillas are soft, round, unleavened breads made from corn, flat and slightly browned. They are filled with anything tasty, rolled up and eaten, washed down with beer or good red wine.

To fill our tortillas we can choose from an array of dishes that come from nearly every part of Mexico. This is indeed a moveable feast: *carnitas,* roast beef or pork, crispy and full of flavour, from the north; from Oaxaca a stringy melted cheese, nutty and dry in taste; from the Gulf coast guacamole, with avocados, onions chopped fine, fresh coriander and a little black pepper – a smooth mixture that goes with anything. Flat cactus leaves, with the spines and skin cut away, stir-fried with pumpkin flowers, is a delicate, gentle combination called in Mexico *nopales* and *flor de calabaza.* Another ubiquitous sauce is made from green tomatoes, with onions, a little chili and the fresh green coriander that adds flavour, as does garlic, to everything that is cooked. Last of all we could choose from two Mexican specials. The first is chicken mole, roast or steamed chicken covered with mole sauce, which some say contains up to thirty-seven ingredients: spices, herbs, possibly everything that is mentioned above – plus chocolate. The thick, brown, creamy sauce is richness itself. And then there is *huitlacoche,* an ear of corn that has been invaded by black fungus, stir-fried to produce a dark mysterious flavour that is absolutely delicious.

When the last tortilla has been rolled and eaten, the last scrap of *huitlacoche* wiped up, if there is room, a bowl of *pozole* might go down nicely. This is a thin chicken soup enriched with fat corn kernels, a sharp chili flavour, a touch of fresh-squeezed lime, and sprinkled with grated raw cabbage, raw onion and a little chopped coriander. It has a fresh clean taste that brings the palate back to life – again.

Mexican sweets, *postres* they are known as, are also varied, but less exciting than the main dishes. Perhaps it is just as well. A cup of coffee, a glass of Mexican Spanish-style brandy, full in flavour and slightly sweet, and what often turns up to accompany it – Turkish delight in the colours of the Mexican flag, red and white and green.

After that it will be time to take a deep breath, walk a little in the outside air, greet a smiling face or two, happy in the thought that you are here. Everyone should go to Mexico.

THE UNITED STATES OF MEXICO

State	Area (sq. km.)	Population (1990)	Capital
Aguascalientes	5,471	720,000	Aguascalientes
Baja California	69,921	1,658,000	Mexicali
Baja California Sur	73,475	317,000	La Paz
Campeche	50,812	529,000	Campeche
Chiapas	74,211	3,204,000	Tuxtla Gutiérrez
Chihuahua	244,938	2,440,000	Chihuahua
Coahuila	149,982	1,971,000	Saltillo
Colima	5,191	425,000	Colima
Durango	123,181	1,352,000	Durango
Guanajuato	30,491	3,980,000	Guanajuato
Guerrero	64,281	2,622,000	Chilpancingo
Hidalgo	20,813	1,881,000	Pachuca
Jalisco	80,836	5,279,000	Guadalajara
Mexico	21,355	9,816,000	Toluca
Michoacán	59,928	3,534,000	Morelia
Morelos	4,950	1,195,000	Cuernavaca
Nayarit	26,979	816,000	Tepic
Nuevo León	64,924	3,086,000	Monterrey
Oaxaca	93,952	3,022,000	Oaxaca
Puebla	33,902	4,118,000	Puebla
Querétaro	11,499	1,044,000	Querétaro
Quintana Roo	50,212	494,000	Chetumal
San Luis Potosí	63,068	2,002,000	San Luis Potosí
Sinaloa	58,328	2,211,000	Culiacán
Sonora	182,052	1,822,000	Hermosillo
Tabasco	25,267	1,501,000	Villahermosa
Tamaulipas	79,384	2,224,000	Cuidad Victoria
Tlaxcala	4,016	764,000	Tlaxcala
Veracruz	71,699	6,215,000	Xalapa Enríquez
Yucatán	38,402	1,364,000	Mérida
Zacatecas	73,252	1,278,000	Zacatecas
Mexico City D.F.	1,479	8,237,000	

CHRONOLOGY

1200-1300 BC	Olmec domination
100-900 AD	Teotihuacán domination
900-1300	Toltec domination
1325-1521	Mexica-Aztec domination
1517	First recorded sighting of Mexico
1518	Expedition of Juan de Grijalva
1519	Cortés lands in Tabasco and founds Veracruz
1521	Conquest of Mexico
1524	Arrival of the first Franciscans
1527	First Audiencia under Nuño de Guzmán
1531	First apparition of the Virgin of Guadalupe
1535-50	Administration of first viceroy, Mendoza. Exploration of northern territories and efforts to suppress the encomienda system
1552-91	Chichimeca War
1566	Aborted coup of Martin Cortés
1571	Inquisition established
1591	All lands in Mexico declared property of the Spanish Crown
1789-94	Viceroy Revillagigedo's progressive administration
1810	Hidalgo calls for independence from Spain
1811	Insurgents defeated and Hidalgo executed
1813	Morelos summons First Constitutional Assembly
1815	Morelos captured and executed
1821	Iturbide enters Mexico City and is crowned emperor
1823	Iturbide abdicates
1824-34	First Federalist regime, Guadalupe Victoria first president
1825-31	Presidency of Vicente Guerrero
1835-46	Centralist interregnum
1846	Restoration of Federalism
1846-48	War with the United States, Mexico defeated, cedes Texas, New Mexico and Upper California to the U.S.A.
1857	New Constitution promulgated
1858-61	Reform Wars
1861	European intervention
1864	Archduke Maximilian of Hapsburg installed emperor
1967	Maximilian defeated and executed
1867-72	Presidency of Benito Juárez
1876	Porfirio Díaz comes to power
1906-7	Strikes by miners and textile workers brutally suppressed
1910	First shots of the revolution fired
1911	Díaz resigns, Madero inaugurated as president
1913	Huerta seizes power, Madero is executed
1914	Huerta forced to resign
1917	Constitution promulgated

1919	Zapata killed
1920	Carranza killed
1920-24	Presidency of Alvaro Obregón
1923	Pancho Villa killed
1924-28	Presidency of Plutarcho Elias Calles
1926-29	Cristero rebellion
1929	Calles founds the Institutional Revolutionary Party (PRI)
1930-32	Presidency of Alberado L. Rodríguez. Enforcement of anti-clerical laws continues to cause strong protests
1934-40	Presidency of Lázaro Cárdenas del Rio. Break-up of large estates, distribution of land to peasants and formation of collective farms. Nationalization of railways from British and petroleum companies from British and Americans
1940-46	Presidency of Manuel Avila Camacho. Improvement of education, electoral and social reforms, restrictions of church services lifted
1942	Declaration of war on the Axis powers. Mexican troops, workers and strategic supplies sent to U.S.A. for war effort
1946-52	Presidency of Miguel Aleman Valdes. Development of industry, agriculture, transport and higher education
1952-58	Presidency of Adolfo Ruiz Cortines. Further growth in all areas, but foreign trade imbalance causes devaluation of the peso from 8.65 to 12.50 to the dollar, where it stays for 22 years
1958-62	Presidency of Adolfo López Mateos, a popular and effective administrator
1964-70	Continuing growth under President Gustavo Diaz Ordaz, a man of enterprise and character. Harsh measures taken to suppress student agitation aimed at obstructing the 1968 Olympics, held with great success in Mexico City
1970-76	President Luis Echevaría Alvarez endeavours to impose fundamental socialism on the Mexican economy, with disastrous results. Beginning of a series of devaluations of the peso and serious inflation. 200-mile maritime limit established. Relations with Franco's Spain severed
1976-82	Presidency of José Lopéz Portillo y Pacheco. Rise of petroleum price to $35 a barrel provokes unprecedented extravagance in government expenditure and heavy borrowing from international banks and governments. Its fall to $8 bankrupts Mexico and causes devaluation and high inflation. Nationalization of banks further weakens the economy
1982-88	President Miguel de la Madrid Hurtado manages to maintain social stability, put some order into the economy and raise morale. Negotiations begin for the reduction of the enormous foreign debt
1985	Mexico City earthquake causes heavy losses and damage
1988	Election of President Carlos Salinas de Gortari at the age of 42, who manages to control runaway inflation, privatizes banks and many key industries, and re-establishes confidence in the Mexican economy at home and abroad

Index

A

Acapulco 8, 32, 49, 136, 155, 156, 247
Adams, Thomas 28
Aguascalientes 285
Aguilar 130, 131, 132
Agustín I, Emperor (see Iturbide, Agustín)
Alamo 28, 157
Alasea 54
Albuquerque 158
Alhóndiga de Granaditas 155
Allende, Ignacio de 154, 155
Alpert, Herb 25
America 8
Angostura, Battle of 193
Arango, Doroteo (see Villa, Pancho)
Arizona 194, 195
Asia 90
Atlantic Ocean 27
Atlantis 90
Audiencia Council 153
Austin, Stephen 158
Avila, brothers 153
Ayala, Plan of 204, 207
Aztecs 8, 27, 50, 52, 53, 55, 91, 92, 93, 94, 129, 131, 132, 133, 134, 153, 199, 208, 246, 282

B

Baja California 25, 26, 50, 205
Baja California Norte 25, 32
Ball game (ancient) 129, 130
Becán 29
Belize 8
Bering Strait 54
Bolivar, Simon 241
Bourbons, dynasty 154
Bowie, Jim 28, 158
Brando, Marlon 208
Brasiliano, Rock 29
Bravo del Norte (Rio Grande) 8, 25
Brownsville (see Matamoros)
Burton, Richard 49
Bustamente 160

C

caballiotos 135
Cabo Catoche 8
Cadiz 136
California 158, 194, 206
Calleja, Felix María 156
Calles, Plutarce Elias 206, 207, 244
calpulli 200
Camacho, Manuel Avila 245
Camarena, Gonzalez 204, 207
Campeche 27, 28, 29, 131, 285
campesinos 208
Cananea 200
Canary Islands 136
Cardenas, Lazaro 208, 245
Carlota, Empress 197
Carranza, Venustiano 204, 205, 207, 241
Carribean 8
Catholic Church 53, 194, 195, 196, 199, 206, 243, 244, 245, 248
chapetones 135
Chaplin, Charlie 247
Chapultepec (see Mexico City)
Charles I, King 136
charros 246
Chevalier, Robert 29
Chiapas, state of 29, 30, 31, 32,96, 134
Chichén Itzá 129, 130
Chichimec(s) 26, 92, 158
Chihuahua, state of 26, 50, 92, 205
Chihuahua (dog) 26
chinampas 93, 153
Ciudad del Carmen 285
Ciudad Juárez (El Paso) 8, 202, 203, 204
Ciudad Victoria 27
Coatzacoalcos 199
Colima, state of 50
Colorado 194
Comonfort, Ignacio 195
Córdoba, Francisco Herández de 131
Cortés, Hernán 27, 50, 52, 93, 94, 131, 132, 133, 134, 193
Cortés, Martin 153
Cortés, Sea of 26
creoles 135, 136, 154
Cristeros 245
Crockett, Davy 28, 158
Cuauhtemoc 50, 133, 134
Cuautla 202, 204
Cuba 193

Cuernavaca 207
curanderas 248

D

Díaz, José de la Cruz Porfirio 197, 198, 200, 201, 203, 205
Diego, Juan 243
Dolores 51, 154
Drake, Francis 29
Durango 26

E

ejido (lands) 201, 204, 205, 208
Eliot, T.S. 207
El Paso (see Ciudad Juárez)
El Salvador 96
El Tajín 246
encomienda (land-holding system) 134, 136
England 26
Europe 8, 51

F

Federal District (Distrito Federal) 25, 52
Ferdinand VII, King 159
Fernández, Emilio 241
Fernández, Felix (see Victoria, Guadalupe)
Florida 158
food 284
France 49, 50, 196, 197
Fuentes, Carlos 207

G

Gante,Fray Pedro de 133
Gardner, Ava 49
Gonzalez, Abraham 26
Grant, Ulysses S. 194
Great Britain 49, 50, 196, 197
Greene, Graham 207
Gregorian calender 94
Grijalva, Juan de 131
gringos 241
Guadalupe, Virgin of 243, 248
Guanajuato, state of 51, 135, 154, 155
Guanajuato, city of 154, 155
Guatemala 29, 32, 96, 134, 135, 199
Guerrero, state of 32, 49, 50
Guerrero (companion of Aguilar) 130, 131
Guerrero, Vicente 156, 160

H

hacienda 136, 160, 201, 205
Hapsburgs, dynasty 154
Henry VIII, King 51
Hidalgo, state of 130
Hidalgo y Costilla, Miguel 51, 154, 155, 193, 244
Houston, Sam 159
Huastecs 31
Huerta, Victoriano 203, 204, 241
Huitzipochtli (Aztec god) 92, 94, 282
Huston, John 49

I

Isla Mujeres 8
Iturbide, Agustín 156, 157, 158, 159
Ixtacihuatl (volcano) 50, 52, 89, 92, 193
Ixtapa 32, 49

J

jaguar 56, 89, 90, 146
Jalisco, state of 49, 50
Juárez, Benito Pablo 31, 49, 50, 195, 196, 198, 244

L

Landa, Diego 135
La Paz 26
Las Casas, Bartolome de 135
latifundistas 201
La Venta 28, 90, 95
Lee, Robert E. 194
Lenin 203
Lerdo 198
Limantour 203
limpia 281
Lincoln, Abraham 193
London 200
Los Angeles 158
lucha libre 247
Lundberg, Hans 54
Lynchburg Ferry 159

M

machismo 242
Madero, Francisco Indalécio 201, 202, 203, 205, 207
Malintzin (Doña Marina, La Malinche) 131, 132, 153
mañanitas 53

Marceau, Marcel 247
mariachi 53
Marx, brothers 247
Marx, Karl 203
Matamoros (Brownsville) 8, 27
Maximilian, Ferdinand, Emperor 50, 53, 195, 197, 198
Maya 8, 26, 28, 30, 32, 55, 56, 93, 94, 95, 96, 129, 130, 131, 133, 134, 135, 153, 208, 246, 282
McIlhenny, Edmund 28
Mesilla Valley 195
mestizos 135, 155
Mexicali 25, 27
Mexican National Institute of Anthropology 55
Mexican Revolution 31, 201, 203
Mexica(s) 52, 92, 135
Mexico City 8, 25, 30, 51, 52, 53, 54, 55, 91, 92, 130, 133, 134, 135, 136, 154, 155, 157, 194, 197, 202, 285; Bellas Artes 153, 199; Chapultec Park 89, 92, 194; House of Tiles 156; National Museum of Anthropology 89; National Museum of History 160, 204; National Palace 52, 93, 157, 203; Paseo de la Reforma 203; Plaza Garibaldi 53; Templo Mayor 52; Zocalo 52, 93
Mexico, Gulf of 8, 27, 28, 89, 159, 199
Michoacán, state of 8, 50, 51, 54
missionaries 56, 133, 135
Mixtecs 31, 130
Moctezuma (see Montezuma)
Monte Albán 30, 31, 130
Montejo, Francisco de 134
Montezuma 27, 50, 132, 133
Morelos, José María 155, 156
Morelos, state of 202, 204, 207
Morgan, Henry 28
Morgan, J.P. 207

N

Náhuatl (language) 50, 131
Napoleon 154
Napoleon III 197
Nevada 194
New Mexico 194
New Orleans 195
New Spain (Mexico) 32, 134, 136, 153, 158
New York 55, 200
Niños Heroes (Boy Heroes) 194
Nuevo Laredo (Laredo) 8

O

Oaxaca 29, 30, 31, 32, 130, 195, 198
Obregón, Alvaro 205, 206, 244, 245, 282
oil 27, 90, 200, 205 208, 241
Olmecs 28, 56, 90, 92, 94, 95
Orizaba 200
Orozco, Pascual 202, 203, 204

P

Pacific Ocean 32, 49, 199, 247
Palenque 30, 96
Panama 130
Panama Canal 199
Papantla 246
Paracutín (volcano) 8, 50
'Pastry War' 160, 197
Peten Itza, Lake 134
Philippines 32, 49
Police 282
Polk, James K. 193
Pope John Paul II 245
Popocatépetl (volcano) 8, 52, 89, 92, 193
PRI (Industrial Revolutionary Party) 25, 207, 208, 283
Puebla, state of 50, 51
Puebla, city of 193, 197, 204
Puerta Vallerta 32, 49

Q

Queretaro 192
quetzal 32
Quetzalcoatl (Toltec god) 132
quic 129

R

rancheras 246
requerimiento 135
Rio Grande (see Bravo del Norte)
Rivera, Diego 52, 55, 207
Robespierre 203
Rockefeller Center 55
Rockefeller, John D. 207
Rome 94, 197
Roosevelt, Theodore 198
Ruz, Alberto 96, 129

S

Salina Cruz 199
Salinas de Gortari, Carlos 196, 208, 245
San Antonio 201
San Diego 8
San Domingo 130
San Francisco 158
San Jacinto River 159
San Juan de las Colchas 50
San Juan de Ullua 131, 160
San Miguel 154
Santa Anna, Antonio López de 28, 157, 158, 159, 160, 193, 194
San Vicente Chicoloapan 54
Scot, Winfield 193
Seville 136
Shelley, Percy Bysshe 30
Siberia 54
Sierra de Juárez 25
Sierra Madre del Sur 32
Sierra Madre Occidental 8, 32
Sierra Madre Oriental 8
Sonora, state of 50, 200
Spain 27, 29, 49, 50, 51, 136, 156, 157, 197
Spanish Inquisition 194
Stephens, John Lloyd 30
Stonehenge 194

T

Tabasco 27, 28, 89, 90, 95, 131
Tajo de Nochistongo 154
Tamaulipas, state of 26, 27, 200
Tampico 27, 159
Tasco 194
Tayasal 94, 134
Taylor, Zachary 193
Techichi 26
Tehuantepec, Isthmus of 50
Tenochtitlán 27, 52, 93, 94, 131, 132, 133
Teotihuacán 55, 90, 91; Pyramid of the Moon 91; Pyramid of the Sun 91; Temple of Quetzalcoatl 91
Tepexpan 54, 208
Tepexpan Man (Mexican Man) 54, 208
Texas 158, 159, 160, 193
Texcoco, Lake 92, 93, 14
Tijuana 8, 25
Tijuana Brass 25
Tlatilco 35, 56, 89
Tlaxcala 94
Toltecs 26, 91, 132
Toluca 52
Tonantzín 243
Toral 245
Totonac rain dance 246, 247
Travis, William 158
Trigarante Army (Army of the Three Guarantees) 156, 157

U

United States of America 8, 16, 25, 26, 27, 158, 193, 194, 206, 241
United States of Mexico 25, 29, 158, 193, 184, 241, 243
Utah 194

V

Valdivia 130
Veracruz 27, 29, 50, 89, 131, 132, 136, 157, 160, 196, 200, 204, 241, 246
Venus 94
Victoria, Guadalupe (Fernández, Felix) 157, 158, 160
Villa, Pancho (Arango, Doroteo) 26, 198, 202, 203, 204, 205, 241, 246

W

War of Reform 49, 196
War of Spanish Succession 154
War with the United States 160, 193
Wars of Intervention 49
wetbacks (*pollos*) 25
Wilson, Woodrow 241

X

Xochimilco 53, 92

Y

Yucatán Peninsula 8, 27, 29, 94, 96, 129, 130, 134, 135, 199

Z

Zacatecas, state of 135
Zapata, Emiliano 198, 202, 203, 204, 207, 208
Zapata, Mateo 208
Zapotecs 29, 30, 31, 130, 195
Zocalo (see Mexico City)
Zoquitlan 92